LAST EXIT

LAST EXIT

Privatization and Deregulation of the U.S. Transportation System

CLIFFORD WINSTON

BROOKINGS INSTITUTION PRESS
Washington, D.C.

Library of Congress Cataloging-in-Publication data

Winston, Clifford, 1952–
    Last exit : privatization and deregulation of the U.S. transportation system / Clifford
Winston.
        p.   cm.
    Includes bibliographical references and index.
    Summary: "Proposes experiments in deregulating and privatizing the country's
transportation systems to rid them of inefficiencies and significantly improve their
performance in moving goods and people around the United States; the book covers
roads, airports and airport traffic control, mass transit, intercity buses and railway
networks"—Provided by publisher.
    ISBN 978-0-8157-0473-7 (pbk. : alk. paper)
    1. Transportation—United States. 2. Transportation and state—United States.
3. Transportation—Deregulation—United States. I. Meyer, John Robert. II. Title.
    HE203.W56 2010
    388.0973—dc22   2010026370

9 8 7 6 5 4 3 2 1

Printed on acid-free paper

Typeset in Minion

Composition by Cynthia Stock
Silver Spring, Maryland

Printed by R. R. Donnelley
Harrisonburg, Virginia

In memory of John R. Meyer

Contents

Acknowledgments

This research was supported by a grant from the Smith Richardson Foundation. I have benefited from comments and suggestions from many people. In particular, I would like to thank Kenneth Button, Robert Crandall, Tyler Duvall, Robin Lindsey, Fred Mannering, Steven Morrison, Sam Peltzman, Robert Poole, Randall Pozdena, Gabriel Roth, Peter Samuel, Ian Savage, Kenneth Small, David Starkie, Robert Wright, and David Zipper. Adriane Fresh provided valuable research assistance. Finally, I am grateful to Martha Gottron for her careful editing.

1

Back to the Future to Improve U.S. Transportation

The philosophy of one century is the common sense of the next.

Henry Ward Beecher

From ocean voyages to flights into outer space, new ways of traveling generate excitement because they expand opportunities for travelers to visit faraway places and to reach their destinations faster. Today, Americans' interest in new travel options has been piqued by the possibility of high-speed rail service that exceeds 300 miles an hour and by supersonic air service that does little damage to the environment. At the same time, most travelers would be ecstatic if they could drive on well-maintained roads at posted speed limits during rush hours, fly on airplanes that arrived at their destinations on time, and commute on buses and subways that provided safe, reliable, and clean service. Instead they are frustrated by a variety of problems with the nation's transportation system and disillusioned with public officials who seem incapable of enacting policies that will improve their travel experiences.

Historically, the private sector developed and operated new modes of commercial passenger and freight transportation in the United States and built transportation equipment and infrastructure. Those accomplishments were brought about by some of the nation's greatest business leaders, who were attracted to the transportation sector. According to the Harvard Business School's compilation of 1,000 *Great American Business Leaders of the Twentieth Century,* encompassing twenty-one industry classifications, 102 were leaders of transportation service companies (airlines and railways) or transportation manufacturing companies (automobiles and aerospace).[1]

1. For the complete list, see www.hbs.edu/leadership/database.

Wright and Murphy (2009) compiled data indicating that by 1860 at least 7,000 private U.S. corporations had formed to operate bridges, canals, ferries, railroads, and roads. Total private capital investment in those transportation facilities and services amounted to roughly $3 billion (in 1860 dollars), a significant share of the gross domestic product (GDP).[2] Most government investment in transportation was in local bridges, roads, and, in some states, canals. Klein and Majewski (2006) report that cumulative private sector investment in turnpike construction from 1800 to 1830 in New England and Middle Atlantic states amounted to 6.2 percent of those states' 1830 GDP. By comparison, spending between 1956 and 1995 by all levels of government to build the Dwight D. Eisenhower National System of Interstate and Defense Highways amounted to 4.3 percent of 1996 GDP.

Over time, however, all levels of government became increasingly involved in regulating, and in some cases operating and owning, transportation modes and infrastructure. The trend culminated in the post–World War II period with the creation of the federal Interstate Highway System. In the late 1970s, as part of a broader movement away from government intervention in the economy, the pendulum began to swing back when Congress partially deregulated most intercity transportation services. Since then, policymakers have pursued "partnerships" with the private sector in an effort to raise funds to maintain highways and airports and to build new transportation infrastructure. In essence, the United States has been trying to find an optimal mix of public and private sector involvement in transportation since its founding.

Do the current problems with the transportation system suggest that the nation should find a new stable equilibrium that will persist indefinitely? The unequivocal answer in this book is yes—namely, by designing experiments, which if successful, could take the United States back to the future by privatizing and deregulating the vast majority of the transportation system and by reducing the government's primary role in this sector to mitigating externalities, such as emissions, and to enforcing the antitrust laws.

I am not prepared to unconditionally call for privatization and deregulation because such a major change in public policy is likely to create good and bad unintended consequences. Accordingly, I recommend trying the policy in a few places to see what happens before implementing it nationwide.

---

2. Wright and Murphy (2009) note that $1 billion was a significant amount of money in the first half of the nineteenth century. As a relative share of GDP, $1 billion in 1860 was worth approximately $3.2 trillion in 2007.

Policymakers should select transportation services in certain locales that are provided by the public sector, allow private firms to innovate in those services, and respond according to the results. By producing greater understanding of how market forces could allocate transportation resources, the experiments could guide widespread implementation of and justification for a new approach to transportation policy that could significantly improve the system's performance.

To be sure, it will take time and careful analysis for such a bold proposal to gain support among the public and policymakers and to be properly implemented. But addressing the anticipated political resistance and intellectual challenge to launching experiments will ultimately strengthen their design and improve their long-run chances for success. By developing an initial overview of the economic case for privatizing and deregulating the transportation system, I hope to show that fundamental policy reform is essential for ridding the system of its vast and intractable inefficiencies that have accumulated under decades of public sector management and control.

The Stakes: Transportation in the U.S. Economy

Automobiles and jet aircraft are commonly listed among the greatest human inventions of all time,[3] while the U.S. road system represents the nation's largest civilian public investment, valued at $2.4 trillion in 2006.[4]

These and other transportation inventions and investments have contributed significantly to U.S. economic growth by enabling firms to expand the size and scope of their markets. For example, if a more efficient road system enables a firm to serve regional markets as well as local ones, then the firm can improve its efficiency by realizing greater economies of scale, economies of scope (multiproduct production), and economies of multiplant operations. In addition, the improved road system can enable a firm to reduce its inventories because it receives faster and more reliable shipments of intermediate goods, to reduce its input costs, and to improve labor productivity by expanding its choice of workers and a worker's choice of employers. Households also gain by being better able to optimize their residential and workplace locations. And by reducing the costs of international trade, an improved road system further expands firms' markets and increases consumer welfare.

3. See, for example, www.greatachievements.org.
4. Bureau of Economic Analysis, U.S. Department of Commerce (www.bea.gov/).

In a conventional economic growth model where technological change raises the standard of living, transportation can be characterized as improving the technology firms use to produce and distribute their products and services. Indeed Krugman (2009) argues that the railroads contributed to a fundamental change in the U.S. economy—differentiating it into a farm belt and a manufacturing belt—by decreasing transportation costs. Transportation also promotes agglomeration economies that facilitate pooling labor and transferring information and ideas in metropolitan areas, which are additional sources of economic growth (Glaeser and Gottlieb 2009; Jones and Romer 2010). An inefficient urban transportation system results in sprawl that can limit agglomeration economies.

Unfortunately, a precise estimate of how much the U.S. transportation system contributes to the nation's economic growth is difficult to obtain. Denison (1985) constructed estimates of the determinants of growth and concluded that the gains from economies of scale, which as noted are largely facilitated by transportation, accounted for nearly 11 percent of the annual growth rate of national income in nonresidential business from 1929 to 1982. Some transportation case studies have found that metropolitan employment growth is promoted by greater airport activity (Brueckner 2003; Green 2006) and by additions to the highway capital stock (Duranton and Turner 2008).

Transportation's importance to the U.S. economy is more clearly indicated by its large share of economic activity, as measured by its share of GDP. As shown in table 1-1, in 2006 American consumers spent roughly $1.1 trillion commuting to work, traveling for pleasure, and buying and operating vehicles. Firms spent roughly $1 trillion shipping products to distribution centers and retail outlets, sending their employees to meet with customers and suppliers, and buying and operating vehicles (spending by firms on their employees' travel is included with consumers' transportation services). Local, state, and federal government spending on transportation infrastructure and services contributed $256 billion and upped total spending on transportation to more than $2.3 trillion, or roughly 17.5 percent of 2006 GDP.

Transportation also requires users to expend their time—a valuable commodity excluded from GDP. Table 1-1 indicates that in 2007 travelers spent roughly 175 billion hours in transit, and commodities shipped by surface and air freight absorbed 25.6 billion ton-days in transit. To convert those transit times into dollar figures, I assume that travelers value time at half their hourly wage (Small and Verhoef 2007 indicate that this is a reasonable assumption) and that shippers attach a cost of 7 percent of their shipments' value for each additional day spent in transit—a figure that is bounded by Winston and

Table 1-1. *Total Expenditures of Money and Time on Transportation in the United States*

Category	Money expenditures (billions of 2006 $)	Time expenditures (billions of 2007 $)
Consumers		
Motor vehicles and parts	$434.2	(175.61 billion hours multiplied by
Gasoline and oil	$318.6[a]	half of the hourly wage, $8.69)
Transportation services	$340.6	
Total	$1,093.4[b]	$762.8[c]
Firms		(25.6 billion ton-days multiplied
Shipping goods	$829.6	by the avg. value per ton of $1,213
Vehicles and maintenance	$179.7	discounted by 7% per day)
Total	$1,009.3[d]	$2,172.3[e]
Government		
Federal	$31.8	
State and local	$208.9	None
Defense	$14.8	
Total	$256.0[f]	
Grand total	$2,358.7	$2,935.1

a. To avoid double counting, gasoline and oil should be net of federal and state taxes, which support government spending on transportation. I could not verify that such taxes were excluded in consumer expenditures on gasoline and oil. If they were not, they amount to roughly $50 billion based on 2006 federal taxes and a weighted average of state taxes.

b. "Transportation services" includes both purchased urban commuting transportation as well as purchased intercity transportation, which includes business-related travel. Source: Bureau of Economic Analysis, National Income and Product Accounts, Table 2.3.5, *Personal Consumption Expenditures by Major Type of Product* (Q1 2008).

c. The time that people spend in transit is based on calculations of time in transit for short-distance trips and trips of more than fifty miles, both based on National Household Travel Survey (NHTS) 2001 data, the most recent year for which data are available. For short-distance trips, a constant breakdown of travel time per trip in minutes (for example, trips of 0–4 min, 5–9 min, and so forth) between 2001 and 2007 is assumed (based on evidence of this constant relationship between data published in 1995 and 2001). Total annual short-distance person trips for 2007 are estimated based on historical year-on-year percentage increases in these person trips per capita. To estimate the number of hours that travelers spend in single-day travel on short trips, I distribute that number of 2007 person trips by the breakdown (averaged between the 1995 and 2001 NHTS) of travel time per trip. Because the only data collected on long-distance passenger travel were published in 1995 and 2001, and because the 1995 and 2001 numbers are not directly comparable and a projected year-on-year growth rate cannot be calculated, it is necessary to assume that long-distance passenger trips grew at the same rate as short-distance person trips. It is then

(continued)

Table 1-1 *(continued)*

also necessary to assume that the ratio of passenger miles to passenger trips remained constant through 2007 in order to calculate person miles based on projections of growth in person trips. Furthermore, it is also necessary to assume that the same percentage breakdown of these long-distance trips by transportation mode holds from 1995 and 2001. For each of the transportation modes, person hours traveled are calculated assuming constant average speeds for each mode. Mode categories "water" and "other" are disregarded because average speeds are not obvious and their contribution to the total is minimal. Finally, to calculate the value of person hours traveled in total, for both short- and long-distance trips, total hours are multiplied by half of the average hourly wage based on a forty-hour workweek. Sources: National Household Travel Survey (1995 and 2001); Bureau of Transportation Statistics (BTS) Table 1-39, *Long Distance Travel in the U.S.* (2001); BTS American Travel Survey, *Travel in the United States*, Table 1 (1995); U.S. Census, Average Weekly Wage (2007).

d. The expenditures of firms on transportation are calculated based on components: expenditures on shipping goods, and expenditures related to vehicles and maintenance. Expenditures on shipping goods are calculated from BTS data on total freight transportation expenditures. The most recent year for which data on these expenditures are available at the time of writing is 2001. Year 2006 numbers are therefore a forward projection based on average historical year-on-year percentage growth rates adjusted for inflation. Expenditures on vehicles and maintenance are calculated from BTS data on total gross private domestic investment for 2006 and confirmed by similar data from BEA. Sources: BTS Table 3-7, *Passenger and Freight Transportation Expenditures* (2001); BTS Table 3-3a, *U.S. Gross Domestic Demand Attributed to Transportation Related Final Demand* (2006); BEA National Income and Product Accounts, Table 5.5.5, *Private Fixed Investment in Equipment and Software by Type* (2008).

e. Time expenditure in transportation for firms is based on calculations made for freight ton-miles by transportation mode from BTS data. Year 2005 is the most recent year for which freight ton–mile data are available; therefore historical average year-on-year percent increases were calculated between 1985 and 2005 in order to project forward to 2007. Average speeds based on freight transportation modes were assumed, taking into account wait times, especially important for rail and waterborne freight. For waterborne freight in particular, average speeds are segmented based on where the travel was conducted (open ocean, Great Lakes, and the like). Furthermore, the total number of hauls is calculated for waterborne freight based on average haul length, to which one additional day per haul is added to reflect wait times at port loading and unloading freight. Again, because data on average haul length were last published in 2005, a projection to 2006 is made using an average historical year-on-year percent increase. Across all modes, total ton-miles per day were calculated based on the assumed average speeds by mode and any added wait times. Using year 1993, 1997, and 2002 freight value data, a projection for total 2007 freight value is again made based on historical year-on-year percent increases. Average ton-value is constructed from this total freight value and total freight tonnage. Finally this average ton-value is discounted by 7 percent for every ton-day in transit. Sources: BTS Table 1-46b, *U.S. Ton Miles of Freight (BTS Special Tabulation)* (2005); BTS *Commercial Freight Activity in the United States by Mode of Transportation: 1993, 1997, 2002* (2002); BTS *Commodity Flow Survey* (1993, 1997, 2002); BTS Table 1-35, *Average Length of Haul, Domestic Freight and Passenger Modes* (2005).

f. Federal and state and local expenditures are a summation of government consumption expenditures for the following component categories; highways, air, water, and transit and railroad. Defense expenditures combine expenditures on transportation of materials and travel of persons. Sources: BTS Table 3-3a, *U.S. Gross Domestic Demand Attributed to Transportation Related Final Demand* (2006); BEA, National Economic Accounts, Table 3.15.5, *Government Consumption Expenditures and Gross Investment by Function* (2006).

Langer's (2006) daily discount rates for shipments of bulk and perishable commodities. The result is that transportation accounts for another $2.9 trillion in economic activity for a grand total of roughly $5 trillion![5]

Finally, transportation's influence extends beyond the nation's borders. In this era of globalization, international trade—whose share of U.S. GDP has grown to more than 15 percent—is facilitated by ocean and Great Lakes transportation and by trucks and railroads that carry freight to and from the nation's ports. International passenger and freight air traffic is intertwined with the domestic system. And as a major source of greenhouse gases, transportation is at the center of the global challenges presented by climate change.[6] The United States and other countries face the challenge of simultaneously reducing their emissions and improving the efficiency of their transportation systems to facilitate the projected growth in domestic and international trade and travel.

Certain government regulations and expenditures appear to single out transportation as the lifeblood of the U.S. economy. For instance, Congress passed the Railway Labor Act in 1926 and later amended it in 1936 to force airline and railroad workers to resolve labor disputes by engaging in arbitration instead of significantly disrupting interstate commerce by going on strike. The federal government's recent investments in transportation infrastructure and services have been a critical component of the American Recovery and Reinvestment Act of 2009 (popularly known as the stimulus bill) to spur the nation's growth. Against this background, it is useful to understand how the public sector came to manage, regulate, and operate so much of the system.

The Evolution of Public Sector Involvement

A capsule history of the major U.S. transportation modes and infrastructure suggests that all levels of government have tended to expand—and only recently partly withdraw—their control over transportation infrastructure and services in response to major economic problems. In general, government intervention in transportation increased because of exigent circumstances

5. To provide a fair comparison of this estimate with the value of all U.S. economic activity, one would need to estimate the value of time that individuals spend in all of their activities and include that figure in GDP.

6. Jack Short reports that the transport sector accounts for nearly one-quarter of global carbon dioxide emissions from fuel combustion and that this share is growing. See "Transport and Energy: The Challenge of Climate Change," *OECD Observer* (March 2008), pp. 20–21.

created by private firms' financial crises and not because of well-developed conceptual arguments that justified greater public sector involvement. In addition, as I note later, government regulations often contributed to those crises, and public officials made little effort to help private firms survive. In any event, I do not attempt to resolve whether government's greater role following the initial development of each component of the transportation system was justified, but I do develop the case that the system's evolution with greater public sector involvement has caused it to accumulate inefficiencies that will take decades to shed.

Roads

The first roads in the United States were built by private enterprises; the most important of these were turnpike companies that received a franchise from a state to build, operate, and maintain roads and bridges. State charters specified organizing procedures, capitalization, and par value of stock, and state legislatures set toll policies. During the nineteenth century more than 3,000 private companies operated toll roads.[7] Some of the turnpikes were macadamized or planked and employed grading on steep hills to aid travel for heavier (nonmotorized) vehicles.

States became more involved in roads as private turnpikes failed financially for various reasons, including generous state-granted toll exemptions, rigid toll rates, severe toll evasion problems (Klein and Fielding 1992), and overly optimistic forecasts of how long wooden planks would last (Klein and Majewski 1988). Federal involvement in the nation's roads can be traced to the U.S. Constitution, which gave Congress the power to establish post offices and post roads. The 1916 Rural Post Roads Act authorized federal grants to pay for up to half the costs of constructing rural roads used to deliver the mail. Initially, federal highway programs were financed entirely from general revenues. In 1932 the federal government imposed a tax on gasoline fuel, the revenue from which was formally earmarked for highway programs when the Highway Trust Fund was created in 1956 (Burch 1962). Major federal transportation legislation in later decades significantly increased the size of the trust fund and federal highway expenditures.[8] With few exceptions, federal funding programs have favored public ownership and operation, while

---

7. Klein and Majewski (2006) and Klein and Fielding (1992) provide concise histories of private toll roads.

8. Oregon passed the nation's first tax on gasoline, 1 cent a gallon, in 1919. Ten years later, all forty-eight states had imposed gasoline taxes that ranged from 1 to 3 cents a gallon.

interest groups representing state and local officials, such as the National Governors Association and the U.S. Conference of Mayors, have lobbied for increased flexibility in the use of those funds.

Airports

Private airports, some of which were owned by airlines, were the first airports in the United States. By 1912 twenty airports were in use throughout the country (Wells 1996). Municipally owned airports emerged in those communities that were eager to be connected with the rest of the country. During the Great Depression, private commercial airports experienced serious financial problems and were taken over by local or state governments. It is possible that some private commercial airports could have survived with temporary public assistance and that private airport competition could have developed as the demand for air travel grew in subsequent decades, but the Federal Aviation Administration prohibited private airports from offering commercial service after it was established in 1958 (see below).

The Civil Aeronautics Act of 1938 paved the way for federal funding of airports by authorizing funds to build additional airfields (Dilger 2003). Federal funding subsequently evolved and led to the creation of the Airport and Airway Trust Fund. The trust fund is composed of revenues from aviation excise taxes, fuel taxes, and other similar revenue sources and is used to finance the Federal Aviation Administration's Airport Improvement Program, which disburses funds to airports of all sizes.

Air Traffic Control

The first air traffic control system in the United States appears to have been developed in 1935 by the principal airlines using the Chicago, Cleveland, and Newark airports. The airlines agreed to coordinate monitoring of airline traffic between those cities and opened the first Airway Traffic Control Center in Newark, followed by the establishment of centers in Chicago and Cleveland.

Private air traffic control soon ceased because of the financial pressures brought on by the Great Depression. The federal government became involved with air traffic control in 1936, providing en route service, while municipal government authorities operated the towers at airports. In the wake of increasing air traffic and a well-publicized June 1956 midair collision between long-distance United Airlines and TWA flights over the Grand Canyon, Congress passed the Federal Aviation Act in 1958, which gave responsibility for managing the nation's navigable airspace to the new

Federal Aviation Agency (renamed the Federal Aviation Administration in 1967, when it was brought into the newly established U.S. Department of Transportation). Financial support for the air traffic control system comes from airline ticket tax revenues that go into the Airport and Airway Trust Fund and from general revenues.

Urban Transit

The first urban rail systems in the United States—built by private companies in Boston in 1898 and in New York City in 1904—were given charters by those cities' governments to establish rights-of-way. Private companies also operated the first urban motor buses in the nation. Transit fares and routes were subject to regulation by local or state authorities.

The advent of the automobile put many transit operations under bankruptcy court supervision by the late 1920s. During the 1940s and 1950s, city governments gradually took over private intracity bus and rail systems as intense competition from the automobile accelerated the decline in transit ridership. But Pashigian (1976) and Hilton (1985), among others, argued that private operators could have succeeded (as they have in other countries) if regulatory constraints had not seriously hampered their financial performance. Pashigian concluded that regulation was simply an intervening step to facilitate public ownership. By the 1960s city officials called on the federal government to help support urban transit on the grounds that it would stimulate urban renewal. Thus the 1961 Housing Act and the 1964 Urban Mass Transportation Act gave cities money to buy most of the remaining private transit companies and signaled the start of major federal funding of bus and rail capital expenditures.

Taxis and Jitneys

Taxi and jitney service has always been provided by the private sector. Gas-powered taxicabs began operating in eastern U.S. cities at the beginning of the twentieth century. Regulation of taxicabs evolved from setting safety standards to governing fares, entry, routes, and schedules. Such regulations are not uniform throughout the country; in fact, twenty or so urban areas have deregulated taxi operations (Winston and Shirley 1998).

Jitneys occupy a niche between a taxi and a bus. They typically are small-capacity vehicles that follow a rough service route but can go out of their way to pick up and drop off passengers. Jitney service was first offered in the United States in Los Angeles in 1914. But jitneys never blossomed as a mode nationwide because regulations, often demanded by streetcar companies, compromised service. Today jitneys operate in a handful of mainly inner-city areas, subject to regulations on fares and service.

Intercity Transportation

With the exception of Amtrak and Conrail, commercial U.S. railroads, motor carriers, buses, pipelines, airlines, and water carriers have been owned and operated by private firms, but over time they have been subject to varying degrees of federal and state economic regulation as dictated, in large part, by political forces. With the support of rail carriers and farmers, railroads were first regulated by the 1887 Interstate Commerce Act, ostensibly to prevent "destructive competition." Hilton (1966) argued that the act, which created the Interstate Commerce Commission (ICC), was in fact an incorrect response to the economic conditions of the time. In 1970 Amtrak was created as a public corporation to relieve freight railroads of unprofitable passenger service. Amtrak was expected to be financially self-sufficient within a few years of its inception and to operate as a private entity without subsidies, but nearly forty years later that expectation has not come close to materializing.

Spurred by strong lobbying by railroads fearful of growing motor carrier competition, Congress enacted the Motor Carrier Act in 1935 and gave the ICC authority to regulate truck rates and entry into markets. The Motor Carrier Act also authorized the ICC to regulate fares, routes, entry, and exit of interstate bus lines. Individual states had begun to regulate intrastate bus and trucking operations at least a decade before the 1935 federal act.

The nation's petroleum pipelines were subjected to ICC regulation in 1906, as a reaction to John D. Rockefeller's alleged use of them to monopolize the oil industry. In 1977 interstate regulation of petroleum pipelines was transferred to the Federal Energy Regulatory Commission (FERC). As the ICC's successor, the Surface Transportation Board regulates pipelines that provide interstate transportation of commodities other than oil, gas, or water, such as anhydrous ammonia and coal slurry.

During the airline industry's infancy, mail contracts enabled passenger service to be financially feasible; thus in the 1920s the postmaster general became the first regulator of the airlines. The major airlines suffered severe financial losses after President Franklin Roosevelt rescinded their airmail route authority when they were charged with colluding to monopolize the nation's airways. By the time any carrier started to show a profit, the entire industry had been brought under regulation by the 1938 Civil Aeronautics Act.

Government has intervened in water transportation, including private carriers of inland and ocean freight, port terminals and landside access, and navigable waterways, as it has in other forms of transportation. The Transportation Act of 1940 gave the ICC regulatory authority over inland waterway carriers' rates and entry, while ocean carriers' rates and service have been determined since 1916 through rate conferences and agreements. Ports were originally developed by private investors—mainly shipping companies—but subject to regulation by local or regional authorities (Stevens 1999). Maintenance and expansion of navigable channels is performed by the Army Corps of Engineers. Expenditures on ports are supported by revenues, placed in a trust fund, that are generated by the Harbor Maintenance Tax.

From its inception, economic regulation compromised the efficiency of the intercity transportation system while producing few, if any, improvements. The 1950s system depicted by Meyer, Peck, Stenason, and Zwick (1959) consisted of railroads that provided poor service and earned a low rate of return, airlines that primarily served affluent travelers despite technological advances that substantially lowered the costs of air travel, and motor carriers that charged rates so high that many shippers found it less costly to operate their own trucking service. Intercity buses virtually disappeared from the transportation system. Scholars argued that the common source of the problems was regulation, and some twenty years later policymakers were persuaded to pass deregulation legislation, including the Airline Deregulation Act of 1978, the Motor Carrier Reform Act of 1980, the Staggers Rail Act of 1980, and the 1982 Bus Regulatory Reform Act. Those acts substantially (but not completely) deregulated the U.S. rail, motor carrier, airline, and bus industries.[9]

9. Air cargo regulations for entry, routes, and rates, which were adopted by the Civil Aeronautics Board in 1947, were dismantled by congressional legislation in November 1977. In 1992 FERC Order No. 636 (referred to as the Final Restructuring Rule) effectively unbundled natural gas pipelines to promote competition, but FERC still regulates rates. Shippers can obtain discounts by obtaining "interruptible" service (that is, a pipeline owner can stop service to a customer when demand is high under conditions specified by a contract). Shippers can also resell surplus pipeline capacity to other entities and negotiate rates for storage, hub, and transportation service. As part of the ICC Termination Act of 1995, the Surface Transportation Board was given authority to regulate inland water carriers subject to a "zone of reasonableness" in which a published tariff rate would be deemed reasonable. (Specifically, a tariff rate can be no more than 7.5 percent higher or 10 percent lower than it was one year earlier, subject to adjustments by the Producer Price Index.) Water carriers may also offer unregulated contract carriage rates. In contrast to the deregulatory actions in domestic transportation, international airline travel between the United States and some other countries is still subject to bilateral negotiations that regulate fares and service. Nearly 100 open-skies agreements have to a varying extent deregulated fares and services on routes between the United States and countries in the European Union and in other parts of the world. Fox and White (1997) point out that U.S. ocean freight vessels were regulated, protected from foreign competition, and subsidized. The 1998 Ocean Shipping Reform Act enables carriers to offer customer-specific shipping services differentiated by price and quality.

Regulation of urban transportation persists because federal deregulatory actions did not affect state or city regulations. But are such regulations justified? Are intercity and urban transportation sufficiently different from each other that the government should continue to be heavily involved with the urban system and its infrastructure? Or should the intercity transportation deregulation experiment be extended to privatize and deregulate more of the U.S. transportation system?

Privatization and Deregulation

Government intervened in a developing urban and intercity transportation system that faced different problems than it does today. Regardless of the justification for that intervention, most policymakers, transportation providers, and users have increasingly concluded that the performance of the current system is generally unsatisfactory and that government's traditional solution (reinforced by classic political pressure from interest groups) of spending our way out of the problems is not a viable option because the federal government and most state governments are facing severe fiscal pressures for the foreseeable future.

Privatization and deregulation may appear to be an extreme approach, especially given past problems with private provision of certain transportation services and infrastructure and current doubts about whether markets can be trusted to deliver essential services. At the same time, government failure in transportation has solidified inefficient practices that must be purged and has slowed technological advance that must be accelerated. Private firms may accomplish those goals if they are not constrained by the kinds of regulatory interventions that undermined their initial efforts to develop the system.

Potential Benefits

The essential goal of privatization and deregulation of the U.S. transportation system is to develop market-based institutions that are stimulated by competition to respond to customers' preferences, expand choices, minimize costs, and introduce innovative services and technologies. Privately owned enterprises selling services directly to the public are dependent on customer goodwill and in contrast to public sector providers less likely to have their operations shaped by special interests that substantially raise the cost of transportation to the general public.

The evidence I synthesize in subsequent chapters indicates that the annual efficiency costs associated with public ownership and (mis)management of the system clearly exceed $100 billion, not including the costs of impediments to innovation and slow technological advance. Theoretical and limited empirical arguments suggest that privatization and deregulation could significantly eliminate current inefficiencies and spur innovations that are difficult to envision in the current environment, but the case would be much more persuasive if it were accompanied by evidence obtained from privatization experiments in the United States.

Experiments

Federal regulators obtained credible and ultimately influential advice to significantly withdraw their interventions in intercity transportation from evidence based on unregulated intrastate airline markets in California and Texas and deregulation of truck rates for certain commodities and from empirical studies indicating that intermodal (truck-rail and, in some cases, barge-rail) competition could discipline partially deregulated railroad rates for most commodities. In fact Derthick and Quirk (1985), Breyer (1982), and Levine (1981) argue that intercity transportation deregulation would not have occurred without such evidence.

In contrast, it has been argued that the existence of monopoly elements in urban transportation (public transit and urban highways), intercity highways, and aviation infrastructure (airports and air traffic control) prevents competition from developing and justifies government ownership—or at least regulation. Because evidence in the United States is not available to address this fundamental concern, policymakers and interested stakeholders should not embark on a privatization and deregulation policy without being persuaded that effective competition can develop in those transportation services to assuage concerns that privatization will simply create private monopolies.

Long-term experiments that are carefully conducted by policymakers and that allow the economic effects of privatization to fully develop could provide the essential evidence. Such experiments may be compelling to policymakers in this recessionary climate because they may lead to greater private sector involvement in transportation that could improve government budgets and lead to innovations that spur economic growth. For example, privatization of a major highway would be expected to create a monopoly. But the theory of dynamic monopoly suggests that Coasian bargaining between road users who are represented by a third party and a private highway authority could generate a competitive outcome that enables motorists to benefit from price and service packages that are aligned with their varying preferences for speed and reliability. In the process government would obtain revenues from selling the highway and would be relieved of capital and maintenance expenses, while the private highway operator would have an economic incentive to introduce new technologies, which the public sector has not introduced, to improve traffic flows and safety.

The notion of privatization experiments is a metaphor because I am not suggesting that they would be controlled experiments; they are more akin to the Schumpeterian notion of creative destruction where private operators are given the opportunity to compete with each other to determine the most efficient production processes and innovative technologies that respond to travelers' and shippers' preferences. Accordingly, in a later chapter I identify the key features of specific locations where such experiments are likely to be feasible and where the benefits from privatization are most likely to be realized, thereby generating credible evidence that could help overcome the remaining political hurdles and contribute to a constructive change in transportation policy.

Political Reality

The deep recession that began in late 2007 has significantly reduced the public's and policymakers' confidence in markets and undoubtedly made it more difficult politically to privatize and deregulate the transportation system. Of course, the U.S. economy will eventually grow again for a sustained period, and memories of the recession's effects will start to fade. In addition several factors suggest it is important to look beyond the current political climate. First, as noted, the problems associated with the transportation system are primarily attributable to government failure, not market failure, and the public has become frustrated with the government's inability to improve the system. Second, the nation has been searching for the optimal mix of public and private participation in transportation for three centuries, and it is not going to accept the status quo as a long-run equilibrium. Third, political winds shift very quickly, as indicated by the public's growing concern that the Obama administration's intervention in the economy may be excessive. Fourth, budgetary pressures have made public officials more receptive to private sector participation in transportation, while the long-term effects of the recession have intensified officials' interest in private sector innovations in transportation and other areas of the economy that could spur the nation's growth.

To be sure, overcoming the status quo will be difficult when the costs of change are concentrated among powerful interest groups and the benefits are likely to be broadly dispersed. The experiments that I am advocating are intended to build political support carefully by convincing transportation users, a critical interest group that is likely to be skeptical about privatization and deregulation, that they will be better off. For example, Schaller (2010) argues that a key lesson from New York City's failed effort to implement Mayor Michael Bloomberg's congestion pricing plan is that drivers must be convinced that highway tolls would make them better off. Policymakers could then overcome remaining interests, especially labor, by arguing that the status quo is not a viable option because the transportation system will only continue to get worse given the enormous fiscal deficits and that privatization and deregulation could relieve budgetary pressures and spur innovation and economic growth.

A Road Map

Readers may find it useful for me to summarize my theoretical perspective on the privatization debate and the evidence that I use to develop my argument. The public sector's involvement in the U.S. transportation system is often taken for granted, but, as noted, the private sector initially provided much of the nation's transportation services and facilities that promoted economic development and growth. For example, private ferries, railroads, trolleys, and toll roads (such as the Calistoga road) were central to the rapid development of Marin and Sonoma counties in the San Francisco Bay Area.[10] The fact that those operators fell prey to the business cycle or bad luck or planning was not, in itself, justification for a public takeover.

Indeed, the justification for government intervention and takeover of transportation during the past century is far from clear. One cannot make the case by simply pointing to alleged market failures, such as the existence of scale economies in transit operations, and claim that workable competition was not possible. In theory, market failures should be compared with government failures and how the consequences of each will evolve over time. Periodic financial failures by private firms are not necessarily bad if inefficient firms exit and are eventually replaced by firms that use more efficient production methods and up-to-date technologies. Public provision and regulation may cause greater social costs than are caused by private firms that are struggling financially. Moreover, such costs may be concealed from the public, the majority of whom do not realize the extent of increasing public sector

---

10. I am grateful to Randall Pozdena for this point.

inefficiencies and taxpayer subsidies. Indeed, the strongest justification for privatization may be that it can eliminate dynamic X-inefficiencies—steadily rising production costs and little innovation and technological advance.

Of course, the relative costs and benefits of public and private sector provision of transportation must be resolved empirically. I rely on the available scholarly assessments of the performance of the various components of the U.S. system, retrospective assessments of the effects of U.S. intercity deregulation, and assessments of the hypothetical effects of privatization and deregulation of transportation in the United States and the actual effects of privatization and deregulation of transportation in foreign countries. My focus is primarily on economic efficiency—resource allocation within the transportation system—rather than social efficiency, which considers, for example, the broader effects of the system on the environment. But I do comment on such issues when appropriate. My focus on efficiency implies that I believe that the transportation system per se should not be compromised to improve the quality of life for the working or nonworking poor. Instead, the system should be as efficient as possible, and social goals such as improving the mobility of poor citizens should be accomplished efficiently by, for example, instituting a voucher system.

I stress that far more scholarly evidence exists on the performance of the current U.S. transportation system under public management and the effects of partial deregulation than on the hypothetical effects of privatization in the United States and on the actual effects of privatization and deregulation in other countries. In addition, the extent of the evidence varies greatly by mode and the type of infrastructure (for example, airlines and airports have been thoroughly studied, while inland barge transportation and ports have received little scholarly attention).

I round out some of the scholarly evidence with anecdotal and descriptive evidence from the media and government reports. But because the existing empirical evidence is still incomplete, I conclude my journey by calling for experiments to fill in critical gaps in our knowledge of the effects of privatization and deregulation to help resolve the debate.

Along the way my argument is developed in two parts. In the first part, I motivate the case for privatization and deregulation by analyzing the U.S. transportation system's inefficiencies and by arguing that political and institutional constraints on introducing efficient reforms have enabled those inefficiencies to persist and grow. Major inefficiencies arise from residual regulation of intercity transportation and from public ownership and management of urban transportation and aviation infrastructure.

In the second part, I discuss the evidence indicating that privatization and deregulation could raise national welfare and explain the role of experiments. I indicate why deregulation of intercity transportation, despite constraints on private firms, was successful and outline a theoretical framework for assessing the economic effects of privatizing and deregulating the remaining parts of the transportation system. Based on academic simulation studies and transportation privatization experiments in foreign countries, I enrich the theory with the available empirical evidence. Unfortunately, the absence of privatized transportation services and infrastructure in the United States means that researchers have not had a good "laboratory" to develop persuasive evidence on the likely economic effects of privatization and deregulation. Accordingly, I outline political and economic considerations to guide experiments that would generate actual evidence of the effects of the policy on the performance of the U.S. transportation system. Based on the arguments advanced in the preceding chapters, I expect that the evidence will be quite positive and that top-level leadership will use it for outreach and public education to achieve a constructive long-term policy change that places greater reliance on the private sector to provide an essential input into Americans' work and recreation.

*Motivating the Case for
Privatization and Deregulation:*
U.S. Transportation System Inefficiencies

Intercity Transportation under Partial Deregulation

Regulatory reform—that is, partial economic deregulation—of intercity passenger and freight transportation during the late 1970s and early 1980s significantly improved the efficiency of airlines, railroads, motor carriers, and buses by giving carriers greater operating freedom and stimulating industry competition (Morrison and Winston 1999; Meyer and Oster 1987). Regulatory reform of domestic ocean shipping occurred more recently, and its effects on economic efficiency have not been well documented.[1]

As indicated by the term *partial deregulation,* policymakers did not deregulate every aspect, economic and otherwise, of carrier operations.[2] In addition, they did not reform public infrastructure policies to ensure that each mode's infrastructure would accord with carriers' adjustments to deregulation. In this chapter I argue that notwithstanding the improvements in the efficiency and safety of intercity transportation that are attributable to regulatory reform, the performance of the intercity system would be even better if policymakers withdrew their remaining regulatory interventions—in the process minimizing the likelihood that they would reregulate a mode—and if they reformed infrastructure policies to promote efficiency.

Airlines

When airline carriers were deregulated in 1978, they assumed full responsibility for solving their perennial economic challenge of providing a level

1. Pipeline capacity during peak and off-peak periods has been used more efficiently since partial deregulation (Winston 1998). However, MacAvoy (2000) points out that the presence of rate regulation still imposes rigidities that prevent capacity from being used efficiently.
2. Europeans use the term *liberalized* rather than *deregulated* or *partially deregulated* to indicate that government has less involvement in an industry but that it still has a presence.

of service that aligns their available seat capacity with passenger demand. The challenge exists because of the unpredictability of demand, resulting from changes in the business cycle and unanticipated shocks, and unpredictable changes in the cost of capacity. Unfortunately, the airline industry has experienced staggering financial losses from unanticipated reductions in demand from macroeconomic recessions and the September 11, 2001, terrorist attacks, and from increases in operating costs caused by spikes in fuel prices. Carriers have responded by adjusting their operations and capacity to reduce losses from those shocks.

Airlines have also been under strong competitive pressures to offer low fares, high-quality service, and safe operations. They have succeeded in offering low fares and safe operations, but their financial problems have affected service quality. Policymakers have felt compelled to improve market performance in all those areas, but their interventions have done little to benefit consumers and have unintentionally compromised industry performance.

Service

Elected officials attempt to modify policies that may adversely affect their constituents; hence Congress attached various provisions to economic regulatory reform that were intended to protect certain groups of consumers who might be harmed.

An efficient approach would directly subsidize the adversely affected group(s) with, for example, vouchers. However, the 1978 Essential Air Services (EAS) program misguidedly subsidized suppliers of air service. The program was created to assuage congressional fears that airline deregulation would cause air service to small communities to disappear. Under this program, scheduled to last ten years and to cover 150 communities, annual subsidies amounting to roughly $50 million were provided to carriers that offered at least two flights a day to airports in the program.

According to Morrison and Winston (1986), airline deregulation led to an increase in the number of small communities that air carriers served; in fact, profitable air service without the need for subsidies could generally be provided in the long run for those communities. It is possible that the existence of subsidies may have reduced the potential benefits to travelers in low-density markets by masking the available profit opportunities to carriers. Nonetheless, the program was renewed by the Airport and Airway Safety and Capacity Expansion Act of 1987 and was later made permanent as part of the FAA Reauthorization Act of 1996. As of fiscal year 2007, the annual costs of the program, covering 145 communities, exceed $100 million with a median subsidy per passenger of roughly $100 (GAO 2007). The annual costs could climb to $175 million in 2010.

Because the recent downturn in the economy has caused air carriers to substantially cut their service to small communities, Congress has been poised to increase the available funds in the EAS program. However, this response is inappropriate for at least two reasons. First, for many years, small and medium-size cites, including Duluth, Myrtle Beach, Roswell, Wichita, and others, have used local tax money and waived airport landing fees and other charges to attract air service. Second, additional subsidies may not prevent carriers from discontinuing service after a short period of time (that recently occurred at the Hagerstown, Maryland, airport, for example). Or the subsidies may be used to serve routes with very few passengers. For example, in September 2008 Georgia Skies began air service on the eighty-one-mile run from Macon to Atlanta after receiving a $1.3 million subsidy. The carrier typically provides twenty-six flights a week using nine-seat planes that attract only three to five passengers a flight because Macon airport is "not quite far enough for people to fly to Atlanta Hartsfield [Airport] and then fly out of Hartsfield."[3]

By requiring carriers to provide a minimum daily flight frequency and aircraft size, EAS inefficiencies increase. In 2008 the share of seats occupied by paying passengers, or the average load factor, for commercial airline service in the United States was 80 percent for unsubsidized flights and 37 percent for subsidized flights. The taxpayer should not be used to create artificial profit opportunities for airlines as they adjust their service to conform to economic reality. Deregulation has benefited air travelers throughout all city size classifications who are willing to pay the cost of service (Morrison and Winston 1997). Travelers who live near small subsidized airports have obtained lower fares and more frequent service by driving somewhat further to busier regional airports that are served by low-cost carriers, and new carriers have found it profitable to offer service to smaller unsubsidized airports.[4] In the deregulated environment the Essential Air Services program

---

3. Halimah Abdullah, "Half-Empty Flights Have Some Questioning Federal Subsidies," Macon.com, June 1, 2009 (www.macon.com).

4. The dynamics of airline exit and entry in smaller cities have frequently resulted in entry by small carriers as major carriers have reduced service to those cities. For example, Delta Airlines and Continental Airlines recently stopped serving the Toledo, Ohio, airport, forcing many travelers to drive some seventy miles to Detroit's airport for air service. However, a new carrier, Direct Air, has begun to serve the Toledo airport. Allegiant Air, Porter Airlines, and USA3000 are other carriers that have recently started serving smaller cities.

is not essential and may harm the intended beneficiaries by limiting their travel choices.

Congress has periodically held hearings to enable angry air travelers to vent about lengthy delays, sudden cancellations, and other service complaints. During the 1990s Senators John McCain and Ron Wyden rounded up broad support for a so-called passengers' bill of rights that, among other things, would require airlines to give passengers honest explanations for delays and cancellations. That bill was shelved, but the call for a passengers' bill of rights resurfaced in 2007 following a series of incidents that kept passengers stranded on planes—sometimes without food or water—that were stuck on tarmacs for several hours.

New York State passed a passengers' bill of rights that was thrown out by a U.S. appeals court in March 2008 on the grounds that it would encourage different laws in every state (and presumably create an undue restraint on interstate commerce). The Senate Commerce Committee has introduced legislation, which has yet to come to a vote in the full Senate, that would require airlines to provide food, drinking water, toilet facilities, and other basic services to passengers stuck on planes waiting to take off. In December 2009 the U.S. Department of Transportation (DOT) adopted a new rule that sets fines of as much as $27,500 a passenger when airlines leave passengers stranded on a plane on the ground for more than three hours. The rule applies to planes with more than thirty seats, but carriers have an exemption if exiting passengers would jeopardize safety or security or disrupt airport operations.

The new rule does not appear to benefit travelers. It is likely that a carrier could often make a plausible argument that airport operations would be disrupted, or safety and security jeopardized, if it returned to a gate to let passengers leave a plane. Or carriers may not want to risk a large fine, in which case they are likely to preemptively cancel more flights and cause even more inconvenience to airline passengers. As data become available, research will be needed to isolate the causal effect of the rule on changes in tarmac delays and flight cancellations, the number of travelers affected by each type of delay, and the total costs and benefits of those changes.

In my view airlines are not the primary source of passengers' frustrations with travel delays. The problem lies with the Federal Aviation Administration (FAA), which uses airspace inefficiently by mispricing it, responds slowly and clumsily to bad weather because its air traffic control technology is outdated, and fails to effectively coordinate flights from one region to another. Airports share in the blame because they use runway and terminal space inefficiently by mispricing it and because they have failed to develop effective guidelines for airlines when the likelihood of excessive delays arises. As I discuss in chapter 5 on aviation infrastructure, improvements in airport policies and air traffic control technology could significantly reduce delays and alleviate passengers' discontent with air travel. A passengers' bill of rights and the DOT's new rule limiting the time that a carrier can wait on the tarmac before taking off do not address the fundamental sources of delays— namely, inefficient public policies toward aviation infrastructure—and may cause airlines to unnecessarily curtail service and cancel flights that could have departed without much delay because bad weather did not materialize or cleared up faster than expected.

In addition to air carrier delays, passengers' trips are lengthened by early airport arrivals for security screening. Early arrivals would be justified if current screening practices were efficient and their benefits exceeded their costs. But current screening practices are inefficient and their benefits are surrounded with uncertainty (see chapter 5). Screening inefficiencies have also caused travelers to take fewer flights and have reduced airline industry revenues. Blalock, Kadiyali, and Simon (2007) estimate that baggage screening has reduced passenger volume nearly 10 percent on flights departing from the nation's fifty busiest airports.

Competition

Carriers that are unable to maintain profitability are expected to eventually exit the deregulated airline industry. In fact, airlines such as Eastern, Pan Am, and Braniff have been liquidated and in the past decade, three major domestic carriers were absorbed by merger partners: TWA with American, America West with US Airways (actually called a reverse merger), and Northwest with Delta. But the federal government has been reluctant to allow the market always to determine which carriers should survive in a competitive environment. For example, U.S. bankruptcy laws apply to all of the nation's firms, but they seem to be exploited in the airline industry. Several carriers have gone into bankruptcy since deregulation, some more than once, and some have had spells in bankruptcy that total more than three years. Yet the federal government has shown no interest in limiting the time that carriers can be protected from their creditors by remaining in bankruptcy.

In addition, the U.S. Department of Justice has opposed certain airline mergers that involved a carrier in financial distress, such as the proposed merger in 2000 between United Airlines and US Airways. The visceral opposition that some elected officials have toward mergers was expressed by James

Oberstar, chairman of the House Transportation and Infrastructure Committee, when he characterized the recently consummated merger between financially troubled Delta Air Lines and Northwest Airlines as "probably the worst development in aviation" since deregulation.[5] Oberstar subsequently threatened to introduce a bill to tighten industry regulation if the U.S. Justice Department approves the proposed merger of United Airlines and Continental Airlines.

The grants and guaranteed loans that the federal government provided to U.S. carriers following the September 11 terrorist attacks are still another example of policymakers' efforts to forestall exit. Post-9/11 financial assistance could be justified as a form of "social insurance" that should have been used to reduce the marginal cost of air travel and increase demand. Instead, it did little to soften industry losses, reduce costs, or prevent several carriers from going into bankruptcy.

The government's actions could be supported on the grounds that they enabled airlines that might have otherwise undergone liquidation or absorption to emerge as viable competitors that keep fares from increasing. But Morrison, Winston, and Maheshri (2008) suggest that policymakers' focus on the number of carriers in the industry is misplaced because the carriers' "business model" rather than their number appears to be the critical determinant of the intensity of airline competition in a market. For example, all else constant, a market with three carriers, one of which is a low-cost carrier such as Southwest Airlines or JetBlue Airways, is likely to have lower fares than a market with four carriers, none of which is a low-cost carrier.

Policymakers' responses to perceived threats to airline competition seem hypocritical in light of their willingness to maintain policies that reduce carrier competition. Airport authorities have prevented new entrants from providing service at certain airports by prohibiting airlines from offering flights that exceed 1,500 miles at New York LaGuardia airport and, with the exception of six cities, that exceed 1,250 miles at Washington's Reagan National. The perimeter rules were originally intended to promote growth at Dulles airport just outside Washington, to encourage pleasure travelers to use New York JFK and Newark airports, and to quell concerns that long-range jets could create a noise problem for the neighborhoods surrounding LaGuardia and Reagan National airports.

---

5. Del Quentin Wilber, "Mapping Out an Airline for a New World," *Washington Post*, April 16, 2008.

As I discuss in more detail later, policymakers also reduce competition by enacting inefficient policies, such as airport slot controls, to reduce delays. And federal law prevents foreign airline carriers from competing in U.S. air transportation markets (that is, cabotage rights are denied), while sorely needed capital investment in the U.S. airline industry is limited by a foreign ownership cap of 25 percent. Attempts to loosen the cap to 49 percent to increase international capital flows have met with strong congressional opposition that has no economic justification.

Fares and Fees

To raise revenues airlines have started to charge a base fare and include additional fees for checked luggage, meals in coach class, preferred seats in the coach section, and the like. Because airline fares (and additional fees) are deregulated, the market is expected to determine whether travelers are willing to pay for items that used to be free. However, when Spirit Airlines announced that it would charge up to $45 a passenger for carry-on bags, Senator Charles Schumer blasted the practice and Senators Benjamin Cardin and Mary Landrieu introduced the Free of Fees for Carry-On Act to outlaw carry-on baggage fees.

Flights are delayed when customers try to fit large luggage that they carry on to a plane into overhead bins because airline workers have to collect bags that do not fit and put them in cargo compartments. Apparently, those delays would not be reduced if carriers tried to enforce their own rules about the size of carry-on luggage before passengers boarded a plane. Carry-on fees could actually benefit travelers and airlines by curtailing the amount of oversized luggage that is brought on to a plane, thereby reducing delays and injuries to flight attendants. Congressional efforts to prohibit such fees are unjustified because if air travelers are upset by the new fees, then Spirit will lose passengers and will either drop its fares or eliminate the fee to get them back.

Safety

The Federal Aviation Administration is responsible for monitoring and improving airline safety by promulgating various safety regulations and for providing air traffic control. Air carriers are also subject to the unbridled pressure of the market to operate safely—pressure that contributed to Air Florida going out of business following the crash of one of its planes in the Potomac River in 1982 and that forced ValuJet to emerge as a new carrier, Air Tran, following the crash of one of its planes in the Everglades in 1996. Despite concerns following airline deregulation that financial pressures would force carriers to be less vigilant about safety, the chance of dying in an airplane crash has diminished during the deregulated era. Nonetheless, the federal government has periodically raised concerns about airline safety that have unnecessarily disrupted U.S. commercial carriers' operations.

A recent safety "scare" occurred in April 2008 after Congress learned that an FAA supervisor allowed Southwest Airlines to fly planes that had not been inspected in a timely manner for fuselage cracks.[6] To compensate for its lapse in vigilance, the FAA demanded that American Airlines comply with federal rules about how certain wires in the wheel wells of MD-80 jets are secured, forcing American to cancel thousands of flights and to inconvenience hundreds of thousands of travelers. The problem merited attention, but instead of overreacting to criticism from Congress, the FAA could have enabled American to comply with its regulations without grounding all of its MD-80 aircraft. The Government Accountability Office (GAO) has criticized the FAA's historically inconsistent safety enforcement patterns. Whether those patterns reflect varying political pressure from Congress or periodic "get-tough" cycles, they have damaged the FAA's credibility.[7]

In fact, the airlines and aircraft manufacturers typically know much more than the FAA does about aircraft technology, aircraft condition, and airline operations and can respond much more quickly than the FAA can to address potential safety problems.[8] For example, in 2002 the Boeing Company tested a device to reduce the chance of a fuel tank explosion, which was responsible for the 1996 crash of a TWA flight. It took another six years before the FAA was able to provide a justification on cost-benefit grounds and to subsequently mandate that manufacturers and airlines upgrade their fuel tanks. In the interim, individual carriers made their own decisions whether to use Boeing's device.

The preceding discussion indicates that although airlines were deregulated in large part in 1978, the government cannot seem to let the industry evolve on its own. As recently as November 2009, Ray LaHood, the U.S. secretary of transportation, formed an advisory committee "to identify the most pressing problems facing the airline industry, to figure them out, and have a plan for the future of aviation." In response the major carriers pleaded

6. Southwest paid a $7.5 million fine for operating planes without performing the mandatory inspections.

7. Michael Fabey, "FAA Blamed for Inconsistency in Levying Fines against Airlines," *Travel Weekly*, November 8, 2009.

8. Clifford Winston and Robert W. Crandall, "Airlines Are Safer than Ever," *Wall Street Journal*, April 19, 2008.

with the Obama administration to resist any calls to reregulate or otherwise intervene in their operations—even in an attempt to ensure the industry's viability. Whether policymakers have good intentions or are responding to political pressure, they have introduced ineffective policies to improve airline service, increase competition, and enhance safety, while missing opportunities to enact policies that would achieve those goals.

Railroads

Government's ongoing interventions in rail transportation raise concerns that freight service could be subjected to some form of counterproductive reregulation and that passenger service could receive much greater public subsidies that are not economically justified.

Freight Rates

Regulatory reform did not completely deregulate railroad freight rates. Because policymakers and shippers believed that a railroad could exercise market power for shipments of certain commodities, such as coal and grain, the Surface Transportation Board (STB)—the successor to the Interstate Commerce Commission (ICC)—was given the authority to determine the legality of rail rates in accordance with maximum rate regulations. Under those guidelines, shippers can challenge a rate if it exceeds 180 percent of variable costs and if the railroad in question has no effective competition.[9]

Maximum rate guidelines, however, have not led to a satisfactory resolution of the so-called captive shipper problem that arises when a shipping firm is captive to one railroad and its goods cannot easily move by truck or barge. Shippers, and various organizations that represent them, complain that rail rates are not always reasonable—that is, shippers are paying more than their fair share of rail's costs—and that the STB's costly, complex, and time-consuming rate complaint process results in few successful challenges. The rail industry points out that although its financial performance has improved since regulatory reform, its return on investment falls short of its cost of capital; thus, the railroads argue, the STB should refrain from trying to appease shippers who claim they are captive.

Although both sides have legitimate positions, the dispute could be resolved, and the STB's failure to do so has created a politically charged

9. The ICC exempted intermodal traffic, boxcar traffic, and export coal from regulation. The exemption of export coal was overturned by the courts in 1993.

environment that generates costs to carriers because industry executives devote attention and energy to preventing tighter regulatory control of prices. Notwithstanding shippers' frustrations, Grimm and Winston (2000) found that the loss to captive shippers of bulk commodities such as coal and grain from elevated rail rates, as compared with the rates paid by noncaptive shippers, is small. They conclude that it would be preferable for shippers and railroads to be given the authority to extend their benefits from contracting in a deregulated environment to negotiate an end to residual rate regulation and eventually to the STB.

By negotiating an end to residual rate regulation, the rail industry could substantially lessen the possibility that the board or Congress could introduce new regulations that undermine industry performance. Indeed, Gaskins (2008) argues that the railroads are no longer perceived to be struggling financially and that political pressure from shippers for lower rail rates may well drive the STB to attempt to reduce rates in the future. This prediction may be realized if the pending "competition" bill introduced by Senator Jay Rockefeller and pushed by coal and shipper interests becomes law. The details of the bill have not been settled, but its overall goal appears to alter what shippers have long complained is a pro-railroad stance by the STB.[10] In addition, the Senate Judiciary Committee has recently passed a bill that would give the U.S. Justice Department and state attorneys general new regulatory authority over the industry.

Elimination of the board would allow railroads to reduce administrative and lobbying costs and perhaps raise rates in some markets. In return, the industry could offer shippers some recourse for reducing rates, such as identifying specific situations in a market when an alternative rail carrier would be given access to an incumbent rail carrier's track.

Passenger Rail Subsidies

As noted, Amtrak was expected to operate its rail passenger service as a private entity without federal subsidies within a few years of its inception in 1970. But, in fact, Amtrak has relied on subsidies—well over $1 billion annually in recent years—to keep operating. From fiscal years 1971 through 2006, Amtrak has received more than $30 billion in federal operating and capital subsidies and has obtained additional funding from state and local governments to subsidize corridor routes operating within their jurisdiction (GAO 2006). As a result of the Amtrak Reform and Accountability Act of

---

10. John D. Boyd, "Rockefeller to Introduce Rail Regulation Bill," *Journal of Commerce,* September 11, 2009.

1997, Amtrak operates as a government-established private corporation but does not issue securities to the public and is relieved from having to submit annual management reports to Congress.

Amtrak's subsidies would be justified if they were exceeded by Amtrak's social benefits. But Morrison (1990) estimated that Amtrak's social benefits are highly localized—the gains in the well-traveled Northeast corridor offset the losses in the rest of the United States—resulting in negligible social benefits overall. In a more recent assessment, the GAO (2006) concludes that Amtrak continues to be in poor financial condition and will require billions of dollars to address deferred maintenance. Amtrak also fails to allocate federal funds to improve service in markets that would generate large public benefits by relieving highway and airport congestion. Finally, Amtrak faces significant constraints to becoming more efficient from expensive labor protection payments that could be triggered by possible changes in routes and service.

Given Amtrak's persistently high operating losses, the DOT's inspector general concluded that Amtrak cannot "save its way to financial health" and—in the absence of increased federal funding—may require long-term structural operating reforms such as abandoning certain long-distance routes with high operating losses and few passengers (such as the Sunset Limited connecting Los Angeles and Orlando and the Silver Service connecting New York and Florida). The inspector general also indicated that Amtrak might explore privatization and competition among multiple operators, as is occurring in some European countries.

Congress's instinct is to help Amtrak spend its way out of its financial problems and to initiate funding for high-speed rail. In 2008 federal legislation was passed that authorized $9.7 billion in Amtrak capital and operating grants over the next five years, $2.5 billion in state grants to develop new or improved passenger rail corridors, and another $1.75 billion in grants to develop eleven "authorized high speed rail corridors." In addition the 2009 stimulus bill included $1.3 billion for Amtrak and an appropriation of $8 billion for high-speed rail, and President Obama has proposed an additional five-year, $5 billion investment in high-speed rail.[11]

California is set to receive $2.25 billion—the largest award out of the $8 billion—to begin work on a high-speed system that could extend from Sacramento to San Diego. Florida would get $1.25 billion to build eighty-four

11. The stimulus bill also contains funds for other intercity rail projects. For example, a proposed passenger train between Duluth and Minneapolis, called the Northern Lights Express, is likely to receive what supporters call a "once-in-a-lifetime opportunity for funding." See Dan Eggen, "High-Speed Rail Drives Obama's Transportation Agenda," *Washington Post*, March 8, 2009.

miles of track from Tampa to Orlando. The award to California would represent only a small down payment for a system that would cost some $40 billion, and the "high-speed" rail option in Florida, with expected average speeds of eighty-six miles an hour, is no faster than making the journey by car when one accounts for door-to-door travel time.[12] Very little of the high-speed rail funding is going to the nation's most densely populated routes in the Northeast corridor—a misallocation of public funds that parallels misallocated funding for roads and airports that I discuss later.

Presumably, the initial funding by Congress is only a start on public investment in high-speed rail. Developing a 17,000-mile national high-speed rail network would cost some $600 billion and raise the costs of intercity rail passenger transportation to an extremely high level.[13] Moreover, given Amtrak's limited ability to attract passengers on most routes, the loss in social welfare from a highly subsidized high-speed rail system is likely to be substantial. Peterman, Frittelli, and Mallett (2009) report that estimates of the level of ridership needed to justify the cost of high-speed rail systems similar to those in other countries range from 6 million to 9 million riders in the first year. Acela, Amtrak's high-speed service, which began operating in 2000 in the most densely populated corridor in the United States, carried 3.4 million passengers in 2008.

The costs of developing a high-speed rail system have convinced some members of Congress to explore an alternative approach, which would require the government to seek proposals from private companies to compete for the lowest subsidy to construct high-speed rail service between New York City and Washington, D.C. A privatization experiment in a high-density traffic corridor would provide valuable evidence on whether high-speed rail is socially desirable without committing huge sums of public funds to build a national system.

When the Penn Central railroad filed for bankruptcy in 1970, representing for its time the largest corporate bankruptcy in U.S. history, policymakers, presumably alarmed that unprofitable passenger rail service would spur more bankruptcies, decided to relieve railroads of that burden and created Amtrak. They claimed that rail carriers' rates of return would significantly

---

12. Associated Press, "Gas Prices, Global Warming Renewing US Interest in High-Speed Rail," *International Herald Tribune*, September 8, 2007; Wendell Cox, "The Runaway Subsidy Train," *Wall Street Journal*, January 31, 2010.

13. Audrey Dutton, "Speed Riding the Rails," *The Bond Buyer*, October 23, 2009, attributes the estimate to Andy Kunz, president and chief executive officer of the U.S. High Speed Rail Association. The estimate assumes a construction cost per mile that is in the lower end of the range of cost estimates reported by the GAO (2009b).

increase as a result and that Amtrak would become self-sufficient and oper-ate without subsidies within a short period. However, it turned out that deregulation was necessary to improve freight railroads' financial perfor-mance and that passenger rail subsidies have grown significantly. Unless policymakers dramatically change their policies toward intercity passenger rail transportation, the public will be required to absorb Amtrak's large and growing deficits for an indefinite period and will be well on the path to financing deficits from high-speed rail's huge up-front capital costs and ongoing operating costs.

Other Intercity Modes

Past interventions by the government in the economic operations of (almost) perfectly competitive industries—intercity trucking, bus transportation, and even domestic ocean shipping—are solely motivated by political consid-erations. Today the performance of those transportation services is being adversely affected by inefficient public policies toward their infrastructure and, in some instances, by the slow pace of regulatory reform.

Trucking

After deregulating trucking's economic operations, policymakers have not directly intervened in the industry's determination of prices. The federal government does regulate hours of service for drivers and continues to mon-itor trucking safety, which has improved since deregulation (Savage 1999). Local, state, and federal governments own and manage truckers' infrastruc-ture—urban and intercity roads.

Inefficient road pricing and investment policies have failed to alleviate growing highway congestion and pavement damage. Consequently, truck-ers' costs have increased and the quality of service to shippers, as measured by travel time, has worsened.[14] Winston and Langer (2006) estimate that the nation's truckers and shippers incur annual congestion costs (in 2000 dol-lars) of $2.5 billion and $7.6 billion, respectively. As congestion costs con-tinue to grow with greater truck and automobile traffic, the trucking indus-try is taking a more favorable view of "voluntary" truck-only toll roads as a

14. Despite the vast sums spent on maintaining and rehabilitating roads, truckers are quick to point out major stretches of highways in America with potholes and uneven concrete slabs that could damage their vehicles. The roughest stretches identified in one recent survey include I-10 in Louisiana, I-40 in Oklahoma, several interstates in Illinois and Michigan, I-65 in Ken-tucky, I-280 in New Jersey, and I-95 from Wilmington, Delaware, to Boston. Of course, trucks are the primary cause of significant damage to pavements.

possible way to reduce those costs (Samuel, Poole, and Holguin-Veras 2002). This solution would appear to call for more—not less—government intervention. But as with roads that serve cars and trucks, I recommend that policymakers explore whether privatizing truck-only roads would be desirable.

Intercity Buses

Intercity bus has never had a large share of passenger traffic, but since the 1960s, rising incomes, the growing demand for air and automobile travel, and the decline of central cities have caused passengers' demand for bus service and the profitability of the industry to plummet. Regulatory reform of intercity bus transportation did not immediately reverse the long-term decline. But, as Schwieterman (2007) points out, in 2006 the intercity bus sector started to reassert itself and has been expanding service nationwide at a fast rate with the emergence and growth of Megabus, a new low-cost operator owned by the successful British company Stagecoach Ltd., new East Coast and West Coast operators, and new services, such as Greyhound's Bolt Bus, by established carriers.[15] Travelers' choices in certain markets have also greatly expanded; for example, at least ten different bus companies currently compete on the route connecting Washington, D.C., and New York City and those so-called Chinatown buses are expanding their reach beyond the East Coast to destinations in the South and Midwest.

Unfortunately, policymakers are impeding those positive developments by failing to ameliorate highway congestion and to create sufficient toll road capacity for vehicles, especially high-occupancy buses, that might wish to pay for express highway service; by maintaining regulations that discourage private bus companies from freely entering certain intrastate routes; and by providing subsidies for public intercity bus operators primarily in rural areas (GAO 1992) and for Amtrak that may discourage entry by more efficient private operators.

Ocean Shipping

Coastal shipping handles a small amount of domestic freight, even though U.S. coastal counties hold more than half of the nation's population.[16] Poor public policy is clearly accountable for ocean shipping's weak presence in the domestic freight market.

---

15. The success of Megabus illustrates the benefits to the public of not putting caps on foreign investment in transportation carriers and indicates why policy toward foreign investment in the U.S. airline industry should be reformed.

16. John Curtis Perry, Scott Borgerson, and Rockford Weitz, "The Deep Blue Highway," *New York Times*, November 2, 2007.

Intended to protect the domestic shipbuilding industry, the Jones Act of 1920 decreed that the only ships allowed to call at two or more consecutive American ports would be those that are built in the United States, owned by American companies, flying the American flag, and operated by American crews. Rate and entry regulation also persisted much longer for domestic ocean shipping than it did for other freight modes. Rail and truck rates were largely deregulated in 1980; ocean common carriers and shippers were not able to negotiate unregulated confidential contract rates until Congress passed the Ocean Shipping Reform Act of 1998.

Finally, many ports are congested because charges do not discourage peak-period use of the waterways. In addition, because local regulations and work rules limit hours of operation and longshoremen are in short supply, terminals are unable to operate on a 24/7 basis, as many foreign ports do.[17] In fact, although the World Economic Forum's Global Competitiveness Report for 2007–08 ranked America first in the world in overall competitiveness, it ranked America's port infrastructure eleventh and cited it as a disadvantage to America's overall competitiveness.

Most American costal shippers have turned to trucks and railroads to carry their freight because they have been prevented from buying and using ships made in other countries,[18] faced ocean rates that were elevated by regulation, and have been offered poor service quality.[19] Despite the constraints on shipping operations, it is noteworthy that the industry developed containerization, which significantly reduced the costs of ocean transportation and facilitated intermodal surface freight operations that have grown since rail and motor carrier were deregulated (Levinson 2006).

Summary

Notwithstanding the impression that America's intercity transportation services have been (completely) deregulated, government still has a large—and largely adverse—effect on the efficiency of the intercity system. Policymakers' behavior in the aftermath of deregulation has several implications

17. The Ports of Long Beach and Los Angeles charge a traffic mitigation fee, but they still experience significant congestion.

18. According to data collected by Seasnake LLC, the price per twenty-foot equivalent unit (TEU) of ships built in the United States, including containerships, tankers, and dry bulkers, is at least twice the price per TEU of ships built overseas.

19. Fox and White (1997) discuss how economic regulation has reduced the efficiency of international ocean shipping and contributed to a steady decline of the U.S. fleet.

for developing effective policies to enhance the performance of the U.S. transportation system.

Congress, regulatory agencies, and other governmental bodies involved in regulation have found it difficult to let a formerly regulated industry completely go its own way. At best, policymakers seek to micromanage the transition from regulation to deregulation by instituting certain ineffective policies, such as the EAS program and maximum rate regulation, which are intended to protect consumers who might be hurt by deregulation. At worst, they may eventually institute new policies that, in effect, reregulate carrier operations. Future transportation policies that seek to reduce government involvement must, to the greatest extent possible, result in a clean break between the regulator and transportation service providers. The failure to do so may impede efficient carrier operations and reduce consumer benefits.

The social benefits from deregulation have also been compromised because government has failed to align other policies with deregulation's aims. Inefficient infrastructure policies have limited the ability of modes that use public infrastructure to reduce costs and improve service. Remaining regulations, including those affecting international and intrastate operations, have limited the overall extent of competition under deregulation. Future polices must be designed to maximize the welfare generated by the entire U.S. transportation system.

Finally, government regulation has had long-run adverse effects on the use of labor and capital. It takes many years for the transportation system to rid itself of inefficient practices that have developed under decades of regulation. Specifically, by protecting carriers from competition that would have reduced prices, regulation caused management and labor to develop a rent-sharing relationship that resulted in intense bargaining over what was thought to be an enlarged pie of profits. Deregulation shrank most rents, but labor and management still quibble over the smaller pie, causing certain legacy, or previously regulated, firms to be less competitive in the deregulated environment because of strained labor relations. New entrants therefore have a potential competitive advantage because they are more entrepreneurial than the legacy firms are and have never developed a rent-sharing relationship with their labor force.

Turning to capital, regulated transportation firms failed to develop innovative operations and services and efficient networks; thus they exhibited a lack of technological change and had low productivity growth. As noted by Morrison and Winston (1999), Gallamore (1999), and others, the partially deregulated transportation industries have become more innovative, but they are still trying to shed the inefficiencies of a capital structure imposed by regulators.

As I discuss in greater detail in later chapters, the long-run adverse effects of regulation on transportation firms' labor relations, operations, and innovative activity will be even more apparent if transportation activities that are currently managed and performed by the public sector are privatized. Based on the difficulties that private regulated firms have experienced as they attempt to introduce entrepreneurship and adjust to competition unleashed by deregulation, enterprises that were formerly in the public sector are likely to find that their adjustments to a competitive market environment are even more difficult and take much longer. The challenges that such firms experience—as well as the challenges faced by new private entrants—should not be interpreted as indicating shortcomings of privatization and deregulation. Rather, they indicate the extent and depth of the inefficiencies that have developed under regulation and public ownership and management.

3
Highways

Valued at $2.4 trillion in 2006, roads represent the largest public sector investment in the United States.[1] Consisting of some 8.4 million lane-miles of interstates, highways, and innumerable local streets, the nation's road network is vital to the American economy: 75 percent of goods are transported by truck, and 90 percent of commutes to work are made in private automobiles and public buses.[2] It would not be an overstatement to characterize public roads as the arterial network of the United States.

Given the road system's importance, the worsening strains on highway capacity and durability are troubling (National Surface Transportation Infrastructure Financing Commission 2008). Estimates of the annual costs of congestion, approaching $100 billion, are publicized in *Urban Mobility Reports* periodically issued by the Texas Transportation Institute, but they tell only part of the story. In addition to the well-known costs to motorists, truckers, and firms in travel time delays, wasted fuel, productivity losses, and reduced reliability, traffic congestion contributes to sprawl, lower employment, and carbon emissions, and may even damage the health of infants.

Despite frustratingly frequent lane closures for road repairs, highway crews cannot seem to outpace the rate of pavement deterioration; over half

---

1. This figure is from the Bureau of Economic Analysis, U.S. Department of Commerce. The value of federally owned roads and highways is $54 billion, and the value of state and locally owned roads and highways is $2.307 trillion.

2. Lane-miles for the road system in 2006 are from the Federal Highway Administration, *Highway Statistics;* the share of freight, based on commodity value, transported by truck in 2002 is from the Bureau of the Census, *Commodity Flow Survey;* and the share of people who commuted to work by car, carpool, or bus in 2004 is from Alan Pisarski, "Commuting in America III," Transportation Research Board.

of the nation's highways are not in good condition and 15 percent of the pavement on the nation's roads is rated "not acceptable." Twelve percent of all bridges in the United States—nearly 75,000 structures—are structurally deficient (Bureau of Transportation Statistics 2006).

At a time when all levels of government are facing severe budgetary problems, the American Society of Civil Engineers has called for public officials to more than double their current spending on roads and bridges to bring them to good condition.[3] The states are especially strapped because most are confronting large budget pressures for the foreseeable future, yet they must account for an increasingly greater share of total highway spending because the federal government's share continues to decline. States rely on gas, property, and income taxes to finance roads, while the federal government finances its share of spending on transportation from the federal gasoline tax, which has been fixed at 18.4 cents a gallon since 1993 and has been eroded by inflation and greater vehicle fuel efficiency.[4] The recent cutback in driving and the shift to more fuel-efficient vehicles in response to higher gasoline prices is reducing funds even further. At the end of September 2008, the federal Highway Trust Fund's highway account ran out of money (the fund also contains a transit account), hampering the completion of road and bridge construction projects across the country. The stimulus bill will help finance some highway projects in the near term, but the long-run prospects for highway finance are of great concern.

In another fundamental change in highway funding, the general taxpayer has been compensating over time for the smaller share of revenues coming from highway users. As of 2007 motorists accounted for roughly 50 percent of highway revenues, down from 60 percent ten years earlier and 70 percent shortly after the 1956 Interstate Highway Act created the interstate system. Nonuser sources, which consist of taxes and fees not directly related to highway use, accounted for 36 percent of revenues in 2007, substantially up from 20 percent during the first fifteen years following the 1956 Act.[5] Bonds make up the remaining difference.

After providing an overview of highway policy, this chapter argues that the physical and financial problems plaguing the nation's roads have been caused by public policies that have allowed the performance of the road

3. The society's recommendation should be qualified because many of the investments it advocates would produce low returns and reflect special interests.

4. Truckers currently pay a federal fuel tax of 24.4 cents a gallon on diesel fuel.

5. The figures are based on data in *Highway Statistics* assembled by the Pew Charitable Trusts (http://subsidyscope.com/transportation/highways/funding/).

system to deteriorate and that have raised the cost of maintaining and expanding the system.

Overview: U.S. Highway Policy, Planning, and Funding

In 1916 the federal government used general revenues to provide aid to the states to build highways on the constitutional grounds that road funding supported federal mail delivery. Support for highway programs from a specific source of funds began in 1932, when the federal government imposed a tax on gasoline fuel. Revenue from the tax was formally earmarked for highway programs when the Highway Trust Fund was created in 1956. During the 1930s and 1940s, state and local governments conferred power on local authorities to build the first modern expressways in the United States (Perez and March 2006). In the eastern portion of the country, expressways tended to be financed with tolls, while the western states financed untolled "freeways" with revenues from a dedicated gasoline tax. The states also raised funds for roads by imposing vehicle registration fees, and some states assessed heavy vehicles according to their total weight and distance traveled.

The construction of the Interstate Highway System began with the passage of the Federal Aid Highway Act of 1956 and was financed in large part by a national tax on gasoline of 4 cents a gallon paid into the Highway Trust Fund and by a vehicle excise tax. Revenues from the trust fund paid for 90 percent of construction costs; state governments paid for the remaining 10 percent.

From the beginning, the trust fund's revenues have consisted of tax payments made by motorists in each state. But allocations of the fund to states have been determined to a notable extent by a formula that puts a large weight on a state's road miles, vehicle miles traveled, and its payments into the trust fund—but not on congestion per se. As Utt (2007) shows, the system transfers billions of dollars from states in the South and the Midwest to states in the Northeast, the Mountain West, and Alaska. For example, over the fifty-four-year history of the program, South Carolina has received only 83.6 percent of its payments into the fund, while motorists in Alaska have received six times as much from the fund as they have paid into it.

In 1961 the federal government released its influential Highway Cost Allocation Study that concluded certain heavy trucks were not bearing their full financial responsibility in some states but were paying more than their share in others. However, policymakers' thinking about charges that more accurately reflect a heavy vehicle's contribution to pavement damage costs has evolved at a glacial pace.

Since the 1970s the federal government has focused on maintaining and rehabilitating the highways. Revenues for highways have been codified in federal transportation acts passed every six years; up until 1993 the acts raised the federal gasoline tax. States have raised their gasoline taxes to varying degrees. In any case, total real highway spending has increased even as gas and diesel taxes have essentially remained flat.

The federal government took an early interest in highway design by contributing to highway research and planning (Small, Winston, and Evans 1989). One important result of federal aid was the road test conducted by the American Association of State Highway Officials between 1958 and 1960. The findings have been influential in successive design guides for highway construction issued by the organization, subsequently renamed American Association of State Highway and Transportation Officials (AASHTO).

Today the planning, financing, and construction of new highways and the expansion and rehabilitation of existing ones involve all levels of government, including local governments, regional transportation entities known as metropolitan planning organizations (MPOs), state departments of transportation (DOTs), and the Federal Highway Administration (FHWA) in the U.S. Department of Transportation.[6] The planning process begins at the local level, where every two years MPOs submit transportation "wish lists," known as transportation improvement programs (TIPs), to the state department of transportation. The local TIPs describe every project for which the MPO seeks annual funding over the next three years (GAO 1996). The state DOT then uses these local requests to develop the statewide TIP, which it eventually forwards to the FHWA for review.[7] Once the FHWA grants approval for a project, the state can begin construction. Figure 3-1 summarizes the bureaucratic path of highway planning.

The entire planning process need not take longer than a year, particularly for highway repairs or capacity expansion. However, major new highway projects are subject to a host of federal planning and environmental regulations so cumbersome that they take an average of twelve to fifteen years to

6. An MPO typically has little direct authority to own and operate transportation systems but is concerned with a broader range of transportation issues, such as intermodal coordination and highway investments.

7. States' visions for highway investments sometimes lead to clashes with neighbors. For instance, West Virginia's plans to build a new four-lane highway for commuters bound for Washington, D.C., known as "Corridor H," were met with hostility from development-leery Virginia, which installed a stoplight at the state border to discourage drivers from using the proposed West Virginia road.

Figure 3-1. *The Highway Project Planning Process*

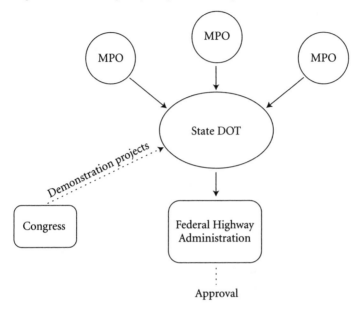

Note: Metropolitan planning organizations (MPOs) annually submit "wish lists" for new transportation projects to their state Department of Transportation (DOT). The state DOT then prioritizes all requests and submits a statewide transportation plan to the Federal Highway Administration (FHWA) that is based on the state's available share of the distributions from the Highway Trust Fund. The FHWA approves the state proposals once it is satisfied that they meet all environmental, geographic, and other federal regulations. Congress can sidestep this process by funding its own "demonstration projects" that are outside the scope of state or local planning.

navigate.[8] Those regulations have the effect of slowing the project development process, because states are reluctant to begin construction until the federal government guarantees its share of construction costs, which can run as high as 90 percent.[9] In addition, even in cases where little federal funding is anticipated, states will follow federal processes to preserve the option to use such funds in the future.

8. Sixty-five different federal environmental regulations relate to highways, slowing FHWA approval. For instance, as reported in the Urban Mobility Corporation's *Innovation Briefs*, "Streamlining the Environmental Review Process," July-August 2001, a proposed bridge over the Ohio River near Louisville was delayed fifteen years because of environmental reviews.

9. As indicated in the Federal Highway Administration's *Highway Statistics* (various years), although only about 20 percent of public road miles receive federal support, federal funds support the interstate system and a large share of the most expensive roads such as freeways, expressways, and principal arterials.

Once federal approval has been granted, states receive project bids from private contractors and select the winner—usually the low-cost bidder rather than the bidder offering the best combination of cost and expertise. The states then front the funds for construction costs, submitting expense records to the federal government for reimbursement from the Highway Trust Fund. To receive their federally allocated funds, states must provide evidence that they have complied with a host of federal mandates pertaining to the project's bidding and construction processes. Those regulations, along with those related to the initial planning process, steadily inflate the cost of constructing and maintaining road capital.

Federal regulations first come into play when roads are being designed, because states must ensure that planned projects conform to federal spending restrictions. For example, 62.5 percent of the funds from the broad Surface Transportation Program (STP), accounting for roughly 20 percent of federal highway support in 2000, must be allocated to urbanized areas (with populations over 200,000) and to rural districts in proportion to their share of the state's population. This STP mandate—only one of many among federal highway programs—forces states to adopt a more uniform distribution of highway expansion across the state than would exist if the goals of state highway investments were to reduce congestion and maximize social rates of return.[10]

The federal government provides some funding flexibility so that a state has the discretion to transfer money between programs, but the different rules assigned to the various funding programs can be confusing and politically motivated. For example, 50 percent of a state's National Highway System (NHS) funding can be transferred easily to the Congestion and Air Quality Improvement Program (CMAQ), while any money taken from CMAQ and added to NHS projects can be used only for maintenance or pollution mitigation.[11] In sum, federal regulations force state DOTs to juggle funds to maximize their use of available federal dollars and often force state planners to jettison promising projects in favor of others that satisfy federal highway spending requirements. Because of those regulations, some states will forgo federal dollars and use local dollars to rid themselves of onerous federal requirements.

10. For example, Katherine Shaver and Lisa Rein, "Va. to Cut Roads Budget by a Third," *Washington Post*, May 16, 2002, reported that when fiscal conditions forced the state of Virginia to decrease its road budget 30 percent in 2002, fast-growing Northern Virginia saw its road budget cut the same proportion as other areas of the state where congestion is not nearly as severe.

11. Despite its name, the CMAQ program has little or nothing to do with congestion; in fact, Congress passed legislation in 2005 that included a new mandate forcing states to prioritize "diesel retrofits" above all other investments regardless of the severity of congestion.

The states also contribute to the inefficiency of highway planning by frequently underestimating the cost of proposed highways.[12] The most notorious example is the "Big Dig," a project in Boston to rebuild urban sections of I-90 and I-93 as underground tunnels beneath downtown Boston plus a third tunnel under the harbor to Logan Airport. Although the project was originally forecast to cost $2.3 billion in 1984, the total cost ballooned to $15 billion, making it the most expensive public works project in U.S. history. When confronted in 2000 with the ongoing cost overruns, the chief of the Big Dig project, Andrew Natsios, shrugged, "We can't just leave a giant hole in the middle of Boston."[13]

Indeed, the Big Dig illustrates the large inefficiencies associated with the mutable-cost contracts, as opposed to true fixed-price contracts, that are pervasive in highway construction. As Lepatner, Jacobson, and Wright (2007) point out, although highway contracts are highly competitive at the bid stage, once a contractor is awarded a contract, it effectively becomes a monopolist that may attempt to recoup through change orders the profits denied to it by the bidding process.[14]

Although the actual planning of highways is usually left to the states and MPOs, Congress has increasingly involved itself directly through "demonstration projects" or "high-priority projects," which receive earmarked funds in long-term transportation bills. Demonstration projects were originally intended in the 1970s to fund experimental and promising highway technologies or management techniques, but beginning with the 1987 Surface Transportation and Uniform Relocation Assistance Act, they became a broad tool for influential legislators to bring transportation dollars, better known as earmarks or pork barrel spending, back to their district.[15] The 1997

---

12. Dewatripont and Legros (2005) outline a theoretical argument that cost overruns may represent an (efficient) equilibrium under uncertainty. I am dubious that empirical evidence would show that the cost overruns that occur in practice are justified on efficiency grounds.

13. Christine MacDonald, "Driven to Excess," *Dallas Morning News,* May 30, 2000.

14. Corruption and mismanagement are also serious problems after a contract is awarded. Big engineering firms, including Bechtel and Parsons Brinckerhoff, paid hundreds of millions of dollars to settle charges of mismanaging the Big Dig project. Modern Continental Corporation, the largest Big Dig contractor, pleaded guilty to overbilling and constructing defective parts of the project and faced fines of some $20 million. But the company declared bankruptcy after it was charged and claims to have no money to pay the fines.

15. Retired representative Bud Shuster (D-Pa.), the former chairman of the House Transportation and Infrastructure Committee, was known on the Hill as the "prince of pork" because of his ability to bring road projects to Pennsylvania—the state received some $57 million in obligations for high-priority road projects in fiscal year 2000, almost $20 million more than any other state (U.S. General Accounting Office, "Federal Highway Funding by Program and Type of Roadway, with Related Safety Data," letter to U.S. Representative Frank Wolf, July 16, 2001).

Transportation Equity Act for the 21st Century was larded with some $9 billion of pork, and the 2005 Safe, Accountable, Flexible, Efficient Transportation Equity Act contains some $24 billion worth of earmarked projects.

Some states are leery of demonstration projects because funding allocations are based on congressional horse trading rather than thoughtful long-term planning. Caltrans, the transportation department of California, has explicitly asked Congress *not* to fund any demonstration projects within the state because doing so would conflict with its strategic development plans.[16] Other states sometimes choose not to build the demonstration projects that Congress grants them, even though they forgo the four-to-one matching grants that the federal government offers. Because earmarks represent roughly 20 percent of the total costs of a project, billions of dollars of "unobligated" prior-year earmarks remain unspent.

Federal regulations also come into play when roads are being built, and they have the effect of both expanding the labor force needed to manage and complete highway projects and of increasing the cost of completion. The most costly regulations are contained in the Davis-Bacon Act, passed in 1931, which stipulates that "prevailing wages" be paid on any construction project receiving federal funds. A majority of states have similar regulations on the books (Thieblot 1996). In practice, prevailing wage has been interpreted as "union wage," ensuring that highway projects cost the states—and implicitly the federal government that reimburses much of the initial state expense—more than the marginal product of labor, especially in the South and rural areas where unions have little power.

An Economic Assessment

U.S. highway policy—in particular, reliance on the gasoline and diesel taxes to charge cars and trucks for road use and to finance maintenance and expansion of the system—was enacted when congestion was not viewed as a national economic problem and when roads were generally in good condition. Unfortunately, highway policy has not evolved as vehicle traffic has grown and as roads have deteriorated. Moreover, the Highway Trust Fund is now running a deficit after years of building up unspent balances. Highway policy currently faces the daunting challenge of significantly improving the condition and performance of the road system without adding to government budget deficits.

16. Despite Caltrans' requests, California still receives funds for demonstration projects.

Pricing Inefficiencies: Congestion

The gasoline tax is an inefficient pricing instrument: although it is a rough proxy for road use, it fails to take into account the social costs of congestion. Economists have long recommended congestion pricing to reduce traffic delays. The basic idea is that when the volume of traffic on a road is low, every vehicle is able to travel at free flow speed, and each driver incurs the private cost of a trip, consisting of vehicle operating costs and the value of the driver's travel time. As traffic volume increases, an additional road user delays other motorists by causing them to reduce their speed. Under those conditions, each driver's private cost diverges from the social cost of his or her trip because the social cost includes the driver's contribution to congestion, as measured by the cost of the delay (or the value of the additional travel time) incurred by other drivers. An efficient congestion toll applied to all drivers on a congested road bridges the gap between the average private cost of drivers' trips and the marginal social cost of their trips by making them pay for their contribution to the delays imposed on other drivers; hence scarce road capacity is used efficiently by drivers whose marginal benefit of driving equals or exceeds the marginal social cost of their trips.

Using modern technology, congestion tolls can be collected without disrupting motorists' journeys or invading their privacy.[17] Rather than assign a congestion cost to each motorist, the level of the tolls is determined by plausible estimates of what users would be willing to pay (on average) to save a minute of travel time—that is, their delay during a particular time period. Naturally, tolls are higher during peak travel times and considerably lower during off-peak periods. The higher tolls during peak travel periods reduce delays and smooth the traffic flow by encouraging some motorists to either take longer but less congested routes, modify their schedules to travel during less congested periods, shift to public transit, or not make the trip.

Based on estimates in Lee (1982), Small, Winston, and Evans (1989) report that a nationwide policy of congestion pricing would yield annual revenues

---

17. A transponder-reader system is already in use. A reader device with an antenna on a gantry over the roadway uses wireless data or radio frequency communications to read the account number of the vehicle from a windshield-mounted transponder to debit an account or, in the absence of a transponder, to trigger a camera that images the license plate number of the vehicle so the owner can be billed. The transponder costs in the range of $5 to $25. Grush and Roth (2008) describe the TDP road-charging system, which uses data generated from in-vehicle metering units in response to location information received from the Global Positioning System (GPS). Charges are based on the time of the journeys (T), distance traveled (D), and the places where the journeys are made (P).

of $54 billion (1981 dollars) and, after accounting for road users' out-of-pocket losses and travel-time savings, would generate an annual welfare gain of $6 billion (1981 dollars). Winston and Shirley (1998) estimate that the annual welfare gain from nationwide congestion pricing would amount to $3.2 billion (1990 dollars), but the authors' estimate includes the losses from additional transit subsidies generated by auto users who shift to bus or rail.

Recently Langer and Winston (2008) have pointed out that congestion pricing would produce additional benefits by improving land use and reducing the costs of sprawl. Current policy has contributed to urban sprawl by reducing the per-mile cost of commuting (including out-of-pocket and travel time costs) for most motorists, which induces households to live in more distant, lower-density locations. Congestion pricing would increase the per-mile cost of commuting for most motorists and increase density by encouraging households to live closer to places of employment. By allowing residents to change their residential location, Langer and Winston estimate that the annual gains from congestion pricing would be roughly $40 billion (2000 dollars) and would entail less redistribution of resources from households to the government than estimates that are based on the assumption that households do not change their residential location.

These estimates should be qualified because the toll revenues paid by motorists and collected by the government account for a large share of the benefits from road pricing without an indication of whether they will be used efficiently. Benefits could therefore by reduced by government corruption or wasteful expenditures on unworthy projects. A critical question is whether the potential benefits from tolls are more likely to be realized under public or private ownership of the highways.

Annual benefits from road pricing would be even greater and redistribution would be less if spatial responses by firms and additional responses by households are accounted for, including changing workplace and residential locations. And by quantifying additional costs of congestion, recent research has indicated that further gains from congestion pricing are possible including greater metropolitan employment (Hymel 2009), improvements in infants' health (Currie and Walker 2009), and less pollution because vehicle miles traveled would decline (Pozdena 2009).

Policymakers have not completely ignored the potential for congestion pricing to improve travel conditions. "Value pricing"—a limited and more politically acceptable form of congestion pricing—has been introduced in a few parts of the country by converting existing high-occupancy-vehicle (HOV) lanes to high-occupancy-toll (HOT) lanes, where solo drivers can pay a time-varying toll to travel in a less congested lane, and by pricing new (express) lanes.

Small, Winston, and Yan (2005) find that motorists' values of travel time and reliability vary substantially for different types of trips and for the same types of trips taken on different days; thus many road users—not just wealthy drivers—value the option of using a HOT lane.[18] But inefficiencies arise under current HOT policies because most of the highway is unpriced and because the express HOT lanes tend to be underused. Policymakers could improve the efficiency and distributional effects of congestion pricing by offering differentiated road prices to cater to motorists' varying preferences. Small, Winston, and Yan (2006) demonstrate this possibility for a sample of travelers on California State Route 91 (SR91) in Orange County, who have the hypothetical option of paying a relatively high toll to travel on an express lane or a somewhat lower toll to travel on a more congested lane. The authors find that differentiated tolls can be set to capture much of the benefit from pricing all lanes efficiently while reducing the distribution of resources from motorists to the government to a politically acceptable level.

It may appear that congestion pricing has reached a tipping point and, at long last, has been embraced by the transportation policy community, but that would be a gross exaggeration. Congestion pricing has yet to be fully implemented on an existing highway in the United States, and the new lanes that offer value pricing account for only a tiny fraction of the nation's traffic. Although the federal government offered New York City over $350 million to help fund the nation's first congestion pricing experiment in a major city, the state legislature killed Mayor Michael Bloomberg's three-year pilot project to charge drivers $8 to enter Manhattan south of 86th Street on weekdays between 6 a.m. and 6 p.m. Large trucks would be charged $21. Automobiles and trucks driving only within the zone would have been charged $4 and $5.50 respectively.[19]

18. Express toll lanes have been characterized as "Lexus lanes," but the Washington State Department of Transportation collected data on the users of their HOT lanes on SR 167 and found that the four luxury brands (Acura, BMW, Lexus, and Mercedes) accounted for less than 7 percent of toll-paying vehicles.

19. Policymakers have shown even less interest in using road pricing to curb sprawl. California has crafted several versions of a bill to discourage sprawl, but as described by Felicity Barringer, "In California, Sprawl Bill Is Heading to Governor," *New York Times,* September 1, 2008, the legislation seeks to loosely tie billions of dollars in state and federal subsidies to cities' and counties' compliance with efforts to slow the increase in driving instead of using road pricing to efficiently discourage lengthy auto trips.

Finally, as noted, there are serious concerns that the benefits generated by congestion tolls would be reduced because policymakers would waste a notable fraction of the substantial revenues that are raised. For example, the 1982 Federal Highway Revenue Act created the Mass Transit Account (MTA) within the Highway Trust Fund to cover the growing subsidies to mass transit. Of the 18.4 cents a gallon collected through the federal gasoline tax, 2.86 cents are placed in the MTA. Similarly, more than thirty states allocate part of their gas tax revenues to mass transit. In fact, the growing shortfall in the New York Metropolitan Authority's budget for transit has sparked some interest in Mayor Bloomberg's congestion pricing plan because the toll revenues could be used to bail out the authority.[20] As discussed in the next chapter, public bus and urban rail systems are extremely inefficient and do not merit cross-subsidies from highway users. Another questionable use of toll revenues was New Jersey governor Jon S. Corzine's plan to increase tolls substantially on the New Jersey Turnpike, Garden State Parkway, and Atlantic City Expressway to help retire the state's current debt without implementing any fundamental changes in New Jersey's fiscal policies that created the debt.

Motorists obviously need a place to park their cars when they reach their destinations. The large fraction of commuters given free employer-provided parking is in fact receiving an untaxed benefit that contributes to road congestion. City governments that offer free or underpriced off-street parking for commuters and noncommuters may also add to congestion because motorists cruise through streets searching for parking places that are oversubscribed. Changes in government policy that would set public parking charges that vary by time of day and day of week in accordance with the volume of traffic and would treat employer-paid parking as taxable income would efficiently curb those sources of congestion (Shoup 2005).

Pricing Inefficiencies: Pavement and Bridge Wear

Current highway policy does little to discourage trucks from damaging pavement and bridges. In combination with weather variations throughout the year, pavement damage depends on a truck's weight per axle (the more axles a truck has for a given load, the less pavement damage), and it should be covered by a per mile user charge based on axle weight. A further consideration is that road damage from heavy vehicles increases at low speeds because the load is applied for a longer period of time (Hussain and Parker 2006).

20. Ray Rivera, "Transit Deficit Yields New Focus on Congestion Pricing," *New York Times,* August 3, 2008.

Current charges based on the fuel tax discourage truckers from using more axles because heavier vehicles get lower fuel economy. Indeed, some states' highway charges rise with the number of a vehicle's axles.

Small, Winston, and Evans (1989) estimate that replacing the fuel tax with an axle-weight charge would encourage truckers to shift to vehicles with more axles that do less damage to road pavement, thereby reducing maintenance expenditures and producing annual welfare gains that exceed $10 billion in 2005 dollars. The charge could be administered with a transponder-system that is linked to information about a truck's weight, axles, and highway use. (I am not aware of estimates based on more recent data on truck movements or more up-to-date estimates of the relationship between axle weights and pavement damage.) Despite its intuitive appeal on economic efficiency grounds, a nationwide axle-weight pricing scheme has not been seriously considered by federal policymakers.

Poor highway design and road conditions are a major contributor to accidents and fatalities that cost the U.S. economy hundreds of billions of dollars (Miller and Zaloshnja 2009). The tragic collapse of the I-35W Bridge over the Mississippi River in Minnesota in August 2007 brought forth a new round of assertions that the nation is underinvesting in its infrastructure, but it did little to motivate policymakers to focus on how current pricing policy could be improved to reduce the possibility of similar tragedies in the future.[21] In contrast with pavement wear, bridge wear depends solely on vehicle weight (Moses, Schilling, and Raju 1987). Catastrophic bridge failure may occur when a bridge span is filled with heavy vehicles. By efficiently reforming road pricing in two ways, policymakers would reduce the likelihood of catastrophic failure. First, congestion pricing would reduce the simultaneous and slow passage of heavy vehicles by spreading the traffic flow over time and place. Second, an efficient truck tax would include a charge related to vehicle weight to account for a vehicle's contribution to bridge damage based on structural stress. I am not aware of quantitative estimates of the effects of those pricing components on bridge wear; but the benefits are likely to be substantial because efficient pricing would slow bridge deterioration and possibly save lives by giving transportation

---

21. In the case of the I-35W Bridge, a design flaw played a critical role in its collapse. Policymakers have attempted to improve safety by establishing limits on the maximum allowable weight on a bridge that any set of axles on a motor vehicle may carry. The Federal Highway Administration provides a convenient way to determine the weight limits on the Interstate Highway System with a formula that depends on the distance between the axles of any group of two or more consecutive axles and the number of axles in the group under consideration.

authorities more time to diagnose and repair structural problems before they become catastrophic.

Production Inefficiencies

Instead of making effective use of the price mechanism to optimize highway performance, policymakers have pursued an expensive strategy of increasing highway spending. Capital and maintenance expenditures must be made because roads and bridges deteriorate and some highways need to be rehabilitated and expanded, but inefficient policies have significantly inflated the cost of capital and labor inputs that are required to maintain and expand the road system.

Small, Winston, and Evans (1989) argued that efficient design of highway pavement calls for optimal thickness, or durability, to minimize the sum of initial capital and ongoing maintenance costs. They found that building roads with thicker pavement at an annualized cost of $3.7 billion would generate an annualized maintenance saving of $14.4 billion, for a net welfare gain of $10.7 billion (1999 dollars). I am not aware of more recent assessments of highway design efficiency, but descriptive data contained in *Highway Statistics* do not indicate much improvement in the condition of major urban and rural roads since Small, Winston, and Evans analyzed highway design. For example, the percentage of urban interstates and other urban freeways and expressways in fair or poor condition in 2005 has increased since the early 1980s, while the percentage of rural interstates in fair or poor condition began to decline only in 2005 after steadily increasing throughout the 1980s and 1990s.

Instead of building thicker pavements to realize long-run maintenance cost savings, which would not produce immediate political payoffs, state highway officials have preferred to spend less money on up-front capital costs—thus trading off thinner pavements for more opportunities to pursue more politically remunerative projects within a fixed budget. State DOTs may also find it advantageous to draw attention to their worn-out roads to justify requests for a larger budget.

Improvements in bridge safety are not as extensive as they could be because funds for bridge repairs are often diverted to other purposes. The Highway Trust Fund supports highway bridge replacement and rehabilitation. But as Utt (2008) reports, a $9.3 billion gap existed during fiscal years 2002–07 between authorizations for bridge repairs and actual obligations. Pennsylvania led the nation in funds diverted from repairs, and it also had the dubious distinction of leading the nation in the share of bridges that were rated structurally deficient.

Ng and Small (2008) raise another important design issue by noting that most highways in major metropolitan areas operate under congested conditions during much of the day, yet AASHTO highway design standards are based on free-flow travel speeds. The authors explore the trade-offs that involve the costs of reducing off-peak design speeds by narrowing lanes and shoulder widths versus the benefits from being able to add another lane to increase road capacity during peak travel periods. In cases where peak-period traffic volumes are much greater than off-peak volumes, better highway service—that is, the net improvement in travel speeds throughout the day—can be obtained without increasing construction costs by designing expressways to have greater capacity. Accordingly, policymakers could reduce the cost of delays by expanding the range of alternative highway designs.

An improved design could result from using lighted lane-markers that can be embedded in pavements so that lane widths can be narrowed and an additional lane can be added during peak periods when highway speeds are low. The key technology is called SmartStud, which powers the lights by a single central cable that creates a magnetic field that each stud converts to electricity.

Policymakers have also failed to implement the latest advances in technologies and techniques to improve road quality in the long run. Engineers have found that roads could be made more durable by using innovations such as tack coats between pavement levels and thicker bottom layers of asphalt to avoid buckling, both of which can extend the functional life of a highway at little extra cost. Gillen (2001) estimated that California could generate annual maintenance savings of nearly $900 million by using improved methods for laying asphalt. Smoother roads could also reduce the billions of dollars in wear and tear on motorists' vehicles. But state DOTs award construction contracts on the basis of the minimum bid, not on the technological sophistication of the contractor. Thus highways deteriorate faster than expected because states use crude construction techniques, whose effects become apparent only in later years.[22]

For decades, state DOTs have made visual inspections to assess the structural soundness of bridges, occasionally using hammers and other devices to aid this arguably subjective process. Industry practitioners claim that advanced technologies, including ground-penetrating radar, geotechnical

---

22. Ivan Amato, "Not a Hole Lot You Can Do to Keep Roadways Smooth," *Washington Post,* March 30, 2010, describes significant improvements in pavement durability that result from using patching materials that are made from nonpetroleum "bio-asphalt" or from synthetic plastics. But those materials have yet to be used in practice.

monitoring, static load testing, and structural monitoring, would significantly improve on visual inspections by increasing precision, objectivity, and cost efficiency.[23] However, public sector engineers and managers prefer to use standard procedures mandated by federal agencies and have little incentive to take a risk with new technologies. Improvements in bridge technology also exist but are not being used in practice. For example, fiber-reinforced plastics (FRP) can improve bridge lifetimes because of their strength, light weight, and corrosion resistance.[24] Researched for use during the 1980s, FRP has not caught on because public authorities would incur higher up-front costs, although the cost of maintaining bridges would be reduced over the long run.

Labor expenses are a significant component of both the construction and maintenance costs of highways. Construction workers are needed to carry out capital projects, while administrative workers at the Federal Highway Administration and state DOTs manage the projects and ensure that they meet all regulations. Several regulations relate to labor directly, and they have the effect of both expanding the labor force needed to manage and complete highway projects and of raising the cost of project completion. For example, the annual cost of Davis-Bacon regulations has been found by Allen (1983) to be as high as $600 million (2000 dollars). And similar state regulations have been found to raise highway wages as much as 4 percent (Kessler and Katz 2001).

As of July 1, 2008, the Federal Highway Administration employed some 2,900 workers whose annual average compensation was roughly $40,000.[25] State DOTs, such as Caltrans, with 22,000 workers, have much larger staffs that perform administrative and operational tasks. Including nine other state DOTs, whose employment data were readily available over the phone, and assuming the number of per capita DOT employees for the remaining state DOTs are comparable to the per capita figure for the ten state DOTs in my sample, I estimate that state transportation departments employ approximately 175,000 workers. Counting federal and state employees and assuming their average annual compensation is $40,000, the total payroll approaches $7 billion. Transportation departments are subject to a budget, but those

23. See, for example, Peter J. Vanderzee, "Spend Smart—Not Fast," *Government and Infrastructure*, Summer 2010.

24. Henry Fountain, "Building a Bridge of (and to) the Future," *New York Times*, October 13, 2009.

25. The number of FHWA employees is from the agency's human resources department (personal conversation), and annual average compensation was calculated from data contained in Office of Management and Budget, *Budget of the United States Government, Fiscal Year 2009*.

budgets have grown and, as discussed below, policymakers are under little pressure to minimize the cost of highway expenditures. Hence it is quite likely that the size of the highway labor force has been inflated, at a cost of roughly $1 billion if, for example, I assume excess federal and state transportation department employees are a modest 15 percent.

Spending

As exemplified by Boston's Big Dig, highway officials are notorious for underestimating and subsequently inflating the expense of proposed projects. Flyvbjerg, Holm, and Buhl (2002) found that cost overruns on a sample of large public road projects in the United States average at least 8.4 percent with a very large standard error, indicating that some cost overruns are much greater. The authors conclude that underestimation cannot be explained by error and is best explained by strategic misrepresentation or, in their words, "by lying."

Cost overruns are also common on small projects such as widening a 3.8 mile stretch of Interstate 66 near Manassas, Virginia. Initially a $62 million project, it cost roughly $150 million by the time it was finished.[26] Bajari, Houghton, and Tadellis (2006) find that adaptation costs—costs that are incurred above the direct production costs of a project because of, for example, alterations in the contract—contribute significantly to highway cost overruns.

Inefficient highway spending is also a by-product of earmarked projects that have become a growing political cost of ensuring that multiyear federal transportation bills are passed.[27] As noted, the cost of those projects amounted to $24 billion in the 2005 transportation act. Spending inefficiencies also arise because the distribution of funds within and among states is determined by formulas that produce allocations that are not based on cost-benefit considerations. Winston and Langer (2006) asked the following question: How could highway authorities minimize total highway costs, accounting for users' congestion costs and states' highway expenditures, subject to maintaining the current level of highway spending? They found that highway spending would be much more effective in reducing road users' congestion costs if expenditures were explicitly targeted to those areas of the country with the greatest congestion.

26. Steven Ginsberg, "Digging Deep for Road Work," *Washington Post*, February 17, 2005, and Virginia Department of Transportation.

27. As Roth (2006) points out, the existence of government-conferred rents can be used as leverage to create new rents. In the case of highways, President Ronald Reagan's veto of federal funds for the Big Dig was narrowly overridden, in part because of support from Senator Terry Sanford of North Carolina, who received reciprocal support for tobacco subsidies for his state.

Additional public sector mechanisms, if enacted, have the potential to result in more wasteful spending on highway infrastructure. In 2007, for example, Senators Chris Dodd and Chuck Hagel proposed to create a "national infrastructure bank" that would give preference to large "capacity-building" infrastructure projects including roads and bridges. Under the proposed legislation, most of the funding mechanisms would rely on federal general funds, not on user charges. State and local sponsors would bring candidate projects to the bank's attention—along with political pressure that would influence which projects are selected. The legislation has not been enacted, but President Obama continues to maintain his support for such a bank.

The 2009 stimulus bill provides states with some $50 billion for transportation projects that ostensibly will put people to work quickly. It is too early to assess the merits of the projects that are being selected, but it is clear that politics is playing a significant role in how states are spending the money. For example, Seattle—one of the most congested cities in the nation—is receiving little transportation money because the state legislature decided most of the money should be allocated to other regions in the state. Massachusetts may use some of the highway money it is getting for public transit. Texas is using a large share of its money to help build a highway outside of Houston that is described by critics as extremely wasteful.[28] And West Virginia is using some of its funds to help complete "Corridor H," despite projections that it will be a lightly used road and very costly to complete.[29] Nationwide, the 100 largest metropolitan areas are getting less than half of the transportation stimulus funds.[30] In fact, a basic correlation shows that funds are highly skewed toward the nation's *least* dense areas.[31] By failing to target those funds to the most congested areas in the country, stimulus transportation spending is compromised in the same way that federal highway spending, in general, is compromised.

Innovations and Technological Change

Highway policy's greatest inefficiencies may derive from the slow adoption of technologies that could significantly improve the speed and safety

28. Alec MacGillis, "Money Stimulates Debate in States over Plan's Goals," *Washington Post,* March 9, 2009.

29. Drew Griffin and Steve Turnham, "West Virginia's Road to Nowhere Gets Stimulus Boost," *CNN.com,* March 12, 2009.

30. Michael Cooper and Griff Palmer, "Cities Lose Out on Road Funds from Federal Stimulus," *New York Times,* July 9, 2009.

31. Edward L. Glaeser, "Wasted Stimulus," *New York Times,* March 2, 2010.

of highway travel. The traffic control system in most cities was developed by inexperienced public officials when the automobile was a new mode of transportation. As Todd (2004) observes, in many driving situations all-way stops and roundabouts would be more effective than traffic signals in reducing motorist and pedestrian accident fatalities and traffic delays; yet federal and state officials have not seriously questioned current traffic control technology that inflicts large social costs.[32]

To add to the problem, bad signal timing contributes to some 300 million vehicle hours of annual delay on major roadways (National Transportation Operations Coalition 2007). Signal timing is based on relative traffic volumes, and the data that the vast majority of signalized intersections use to measure those volumes were collected years or decades ago (Atkinson and Castro 2008). The new generation of product developments in sensor, computational, and communication technologies—referred to as telematics—has the potential to make data collection much easier and to provide traffic engineers with continuous data to update and maintain optimal signal plans. Some urban areas, such as Montgomery Country, Maryland, are making plans to install a telematics-based signaling system in a few years.[33]

Telematics technologies are slowly gaining use by the public sector for some applications, such as highway capacity control systems that regulate the inflow of vehicles on a highway. Most of those systems use predetermined criteria to regulate traffic inflow and could be significantly improved by using real-time ramp metering that is based on actual traffic flows; however, effective coordination between the city that owns the streets and the state that owns the freeways and the ramps has not occurred.

Other technologies await widespread adoption by the public sector. For example, instead of using human-operated toll plazas, private highways have been inclined to adopt electronic toll collection (ETC) systems that use an antenna mounted above the roadway to read radio frequency or wireless data messages from transponders or radio frequency devices mounted on a vehicle's windshield. As noted, this technology greatly facilitates the introduction of congestion pricing. But in those instances where the government

32. Todd points out the obvious safety problem at intersections that is exacerbated by traffic signals—crosswalks give pedestrians a false sense of security because many fast drivers turning at intersections are reluctant to stop at crosswalks for fear of getting rear-ended. Todd also reports that officials have attributed 40 percent of the vehicle delays in urban areas to traffic signal inefficiencies.

33. Ashley Halsey III, "Smart Traffic Lights Ease Commuting. Except When They Don't," *Washington Post*, January 5, 2010.

has adopted an ETC system, Finkelstein (2009) finds that tolls are simply raised—instead of varying by time of day to reflect congestion costs—because drivers are much less aware of the amount of a toll when they pay it electronically. The few private toll roads that exist in the United States, such as SR-125 in San Diego, Dulles Greenway, Chicago Skyway, and the Indiana Toll Road, have not used congestion pricing extensively because, in large part, they have been inhibited by government regulations from doing so.[34]

Shoup (2005) points out that a significant amount of congestion is caused by motorists looking for a place to park because curb parking is underpriced by city governments. At the same time, a technology exists—and is already in use in European cities and at various U.S. airports—that would enable drivers to use the Internet to check parking availability before arriving at their destination. New Internet services have sprung up that list open parking spaces in private parking garages and lots within ZIP codes. Such services could also be used to determine the availability of publicly provided curb parking because sensors can be embedded in the asphalt to indicate when a parking spot is empty. And if they are linked to the meters, they could vastly increase the efficiency of meter attendants in enforcing parking violations. However, cities have not begun to provide those services.[35]

Finally, the public sector is limited by current policy from taking full advantage of other traffic-related technologies developed by the private sector. Using satellite information on real-time highway travel conditions and computerized road maps, on-board vehicle computers could revolutionize driving by providing "smart" directions to avoid congestion. The navigation technology could also help road authorities set accurate congestion tolls and allow motorists to know the charge before they reach a congested corridor should they want to take a different route to avoid the toll. Because the public sector has not instituted congestion pricing, it cannot realize the full benefits of the navigation technology.[36]

Further down the road, automakers envision driverless vehicles that can steer themselves and that have the potential to greatly improve safety by accelerating and braking to maintain a safe driving distance from cars ahead and by detecting and avoiding collisions with other cars on all sides,

34. Tolls on the Dulles Greenway are modestly higher, by no more than $1, from 6:30 a.m. to 9 a.m. and from 4 p.m. to 6:30 p.m.

35. San Francisco was recently awarded a federal grant to test Internet-based parking technology with variable parking pricing as a central component.

36. National Cooperative Highway Research (2009) provides a complete discussion of traveler information systems.

and to reduce journey times by driving in tight formations under computer controls that smooth the traffic flow.[37] Successful introduction of automated highway systems (AHS), which can accommodate driverless vehicles, will require government highway officials to work effectively with the automakers. The failure to do so could significantly delay their availability to consumers.[38] In the meantime, it is likely that market forces will do their part by introducing vehicle-to-vehicle safety systems that can alert drivers to the possibility of an impending collision.

Summary and Conclusions

For the last several decades policymakers at all levels of government have enacted policies that have reduced the quality of highway services, raised the cost of providing those services, and wasted public funds by providing services with low social value. Specific policies and their adverse effects are summarized in table 3-1. Their collective impact is reflected in research that finds that highway investments have generated a very low rate of return in recent decades (Shirley and Winston 2004). A further cost, which has yet to be quantified, is the lack of innovation and adoption of state-of-the-art technologies for building and operating roads.

The public's concerns with road congestion, vehicle damage, and accidents that are attributable to deteriorating roads and bridges have clearly attracted the attention of the policy community. Unfortunately, instead of calling for more efficient policies, most policymakers have resorted to the traditional call for more spending. But faced with significant increases in the price of major roadway inputs, such as asphalt, fuel, cement, and steel (Semmens and Romine 2006); strong public resistance to raising the gasoline tax; and a declining Highway Trust Fund balance that is expected to run a deficit for the foreseeable future, the George W. Bush administration encouraged the states to look to the private sector for help. In response, the chairman of the House Subcommittee on Highways and Transit, Peter DeFazio, exclaimed that the Bush administration was "trying to undo 200 years of his-

---

37. John D. Stoll, "Could GM's Salvation Be Stuff of Science Fiction?" *Wall Street Journal,* January 7, 2008; Randal O'Toole, "Taking the Driver Out of the Car," *Wall Street Journal,* March 20, 2010.

38. AHS technology has been demonstrated on the I-15 HOT lanes in San Diego. Liability concerns among state DOTs and automakers are an important impediment to the adoption of the technology for actual road travel.

Table 3-1. *Highway Policies and Their Inefficiencies*

Policy	Effect
Quality of highway service	
The gasoline tax and various fees are used to charge motorists and truckers for road use.	Motorists and truckers are not efficiently charged for congestion, while truckers are not efficiently charged for pavement damage and bridge wear. Thus, delays and physical deterioration of the system are not abated efficiently. Urban sprawl is encouraged because motorists are undercharged for their road use.
The most efficient technologies are not used to construct pavement.	Vehicles suffer damage caused by potholes and deteriorating pavement, and road users are delayed.
The most up-to-date technologies are not used to implement congestion pricing to help reduce delays.	In addition to the costs noted above, emissions are greater, infants' health may be compromised, and unemployment may be higher.
Cost of highway service	
Highway design is strongly influenced by AASHTO guidelines.	Pavements are not built to minimize the sum of maintenance and capital costs and thus require excessive maintenance expenditures.
The planning process introduces many regulations on labor and capital; conformity with the regulations requires costly efforts by administrators and builders.	The costs, including delays and expenses, of labor and capital required to build and maintain the road system are significantly higher.
Costs for highway projects are underestimated, and the bidding process selects the lowest bidders.	Cost overruns for highway projects occur, and possible innovations are not implemented.
Federal transportation bills include significant funding for earmarked projects, and states have incentives to take federal money for low-priority projects.	Projects generate low returns and small social benefits.

(continued)

Table 3-1 *(continued)*

Policy	Effect
Allocation of highway funds among and within states is based on a formula of regulations that is not closely related to the cost-benefit guidelines.	Benefits from highway spending, such as reducing congestion costs, are compromised.
A portion of revenues raised from charging road users a fuel tax are used to subsidize public transit.	Cross-subsidies to transit are highly inefficient.

Source: Author.

tory."[39] The Obama administration has been supportive of increasing public funds for highways, but it has rejected increasing the gasoline tax and indicated its support for private investment in the system.[40] The debate about the efficacy of public versus private ownership and management of the nation's road system is slowly being formed.

39. Lyndsey Layton and Spencer S. Hsu, "Letting the Market Drive Transportation," *Washington Post*, March 17, 2008.

40. Christopher Conkey, "Raising the Federal Gas Tax Is a No-Go," *Wall Street Journal*, March 4, 2009.

4

Urban Transit

In 1964 Congress passed the Urban Mass Transportation Act, paving the way for the public sector to assume control of urban bus and rail transit in the United States. With the benefit of hindsight, it is hard to escape the conclusion that the act has been a policy failure. Although U.S. cities have spent close to $100 billion since 1970 building, and billions more operating, new urban rail transit lines (O'Toole 2010), less than 5 percent of all commutes to work were taken on urban transit in 2004, down from 21 percent in 1960.[1] While ridership has declined, service costs have soared, creating deficits covered by taxpayers. By 2006 annual transit operating expenses were about $32 billion, more than twice the yearly $13.5 billion in operating revenues. Continuing capital investments are swelling the deficit. Capital subsidies in 2006 amounted to $12.7 billion, bringing total annual transit subsidies from all levels of government to more than $30 billion.[2] The recession that began in December 2007 has intensified public transit's financial struggles, prompting a recent congressional proposal for a $2 billion lifeline to prevent future service cuts and fare boosts and to improve infrastructure.[3]

Defenders of transit are quick to blame nationwide trends of rising incomes and suburbanization for transit's financial problems. But demographics

1. Data on transit's share of commutes in 2004 are from Alan Pisarski, "Commuting in America III" (Washington: Transportation Research Board, National Academies, 2006); data on transit's share in 1960 are from the Federal Highway Administration, "Journey to Work Trends Based on the 1960 Decennial Census."

2. Operating expenses and revenues are from the American Public Transit Association, *2008 Public Transportation Fact Book* (Washington: 2008); capital subsidies are from the National Transit Administration, *2008 National Transit Database* (U.S. Department of Transportation, 2008).

3. Melanie Trottman, "Senate Bill Would Provide $2 Billion for Transit Agencies," *Wall Street Journal*, May 25, 2010.

cannot explain bus and rail's declining labor productivity, slow rate of technological innovation, and fares that are set below marginal cost for riders whose average household income approaches or, in the case of rail, exceeds the national average.

In 2008, with the U.S. economy in decline and gas prices still high after a recent spike, total transit ridership rose to its highest level since the 1950s before falling again during the first quarter of 2009. The "paradox of transit," however, is that its financial situation has worsened because fares account for only 20 to 50 percent of transit revenues and its main source of revenue, state and local tax receipts, has substantially declined. Hence, although transit demand is at historically higher levels, many transit agencies are reducing service instead of expanding it.[4]

Increases in ridership also put enormous strains on systems that are in major need of upgrading and repairs. The New York City transit system, which accounts for roughly one-third of the nation's urban bus riders and roughly two-thirds of the nation's subway riders, claims it will need some $30 billion over the next five years to buy new subway cars and buses, upgrade signals, and expand route coverage. It will also need funds for annual debt service payments that are projected to exceed $2 billion by 2012.[5] Recently, New York City Transit concluded that, because of its outdated signaling technology, no room exists on the subway tracks to add trains that could carry more passengers.[6] The agency also found that as demand has grown the system's on-time performance has become much worse; that the distance that subway cars can travel between mechanical problems is much less even though newer cars have steadily replaced older models; and that after spending close to $1 billion since the early 1990s to install new elevators and escalators, those machines are breaking down at an alarming rate.[7]

Other U.S. transit systems have also reported worsening financial and service problems. For example, Washington (D.C.) Metro officials have determined that the transit agency urgently needs $500 million over the next two years to replace worn equipment and to fix deteriorating infrastructure, fol-

4. Michael Cooper, "Rider Paradox: Surge in Mass, Drop in Transit," *New York Times*, February 4, 2009.

5. Ray Rivera, "M.T.A. and Its Debt, and How They Got That Way," *New York Times*, July 26, 2008.

6. William Neuman, "Transit Analysis Shows the Subway System Has Little Room for More Trains. Or Riders," *New York Times*, June 26, 2007.

7. Ray Rivera, "Subway Delays Rise, and the No. 4 Line is Slowest," *New York Times*, July 22, 2008; William Neuman, "$1 Billion Later, Subway Elevators Still Fail," *New York Times*, May 19, 2008.

lowed by another $11 billion over the next ten years to maintain and expand rail and bus service.[8] Metrorail's recent on-time performance and reliability have sharply declined; Metro buses are late more than 25 percent of the time; Metrorail's escalators are breaking down more frequently; and the Metro board has committed to spend as much as $1 million to hire professional "mystery riders" to assess the quality of service on trains and buses.[9] Willis (2008) has recently provided an "oral history" that describes the anxieties that Metro commuters experience because of congestion on the platforms that cause them to miss trains, overcrowding in the cars that creates an extremely unpleasant atmosphere and may cause an entire train to be unloaded because it cannot be operated safely, and disabled trains that force other trains to move very slowly through the system.

The Washington Metropolitan Area Transit Authority has often asserted that unlike other transit systems it lacks a dedicated source of funding. But this assertion is misleading because as of the year 2000 employees of the U.S. federal government, most of whom reside in the Washington metropolitan area, and of some nongovernmental organizations can obtain free monthly subsidies (Metrocheks) that pay for commutes on public transportation. Many commuters who are unable to obtain Metrocheks are able to receive a tax benefit through their employer for using Metro. Those programs provide Metro and its passengers with hundreds of millions of dollars in annual subsidies that are not available to most other systems.[10]

In the midst of its deteriorating finances, facilities, and service, Metro has succeeded in obtaining nearly $1 billion in federal funding to help support a multibillion-dollar extension of its rail system to serve Dulles airport and beyond. The project has been repeatedly opposed by voters and certain policymakers and at various times has been deemed by the Federal Transit Administration to have low cost-effectiveness; but its supporters, especially those who would benefit from having the Tysons Corner shopping area in Fairfax County, Virginia, served by rail, have prevailed, and the extension will be built despite the absence of evidence that it passes a cost-benefit assessment.

8. Lena H. Sun, "Cash-Strapped Metro Needs Millions in Repairs," *Washington Post*, March 27, 2008; Lena H. Sun, "Metro's $11 Billion To-Do List," *Washington Post*, September 23, 2008.

9. Lena H. Sun, "Metrorail Reports 17-Month Slide in On-Time Service," *Washington Post*, January 10, 2008; Lena H. Sun, "Metrobus Success Rate: 73%," *Washington Post*, September 6, 2008; Ann Scott Tyson, "Metrorail Outages on Escalators, Elevators Frustrate Riders," *Washington Post*, March 19, 2010; Lena H. Sun, "Hired Riders to Assess Metro," *Washington Post*, April 25, 2008.

10. TransitChek provides employers in the New York metropolitan area and in the San Francisco Bay Area with easy ways to provide tax-free transit passes to employees.

Recently, the Federal Transit Administration (2009) concluded that one-third of the assets of the nation's seven largest rail transit operators, including the New York City and the Washington systems, are either in marginal or poor condition. The agency estimates that $50 billion in capital investment is required for those operators to attain, and an additional $5.9 billion annually to maintain, a state of good repair, which portends even larger transit deficits in the future.[11]

In this chapter I argue that urban transit's financial and service problems are attributable to public policies that have not effectively responded to changes in residential and firm locations and in household commuting patterns. Moreover, because transit operations are supported by ever-growing subsidies, policymakers have not forced transit agencies to improve their systems' economic efficiency and responsiveness to travelers' preferences (Lave 1998). Instead transit costs have increased, revenues have fallen, service has deteriorated, and local and state transportation authorities have focused on obtaining larger transit subsidies.[12]

A Brief Overview of the Urban Transit Institutional Environment

As Winston and Shirley (1998) observe, the major economic decisions a transit system faces are what fares to charge, what routes to cover and how often to cover them, and where to spend government funds. The policymaking body that is given responsibility for those decisions varies among U.S. transit systems and could be the state, state department of transportation, county, city, transit authority, or metropolitan planning organization (MPO).

Winston and Shirley conducted a survey of transit agencies and found that the power to set fares and determine route coverage usually resides with transit authorities, which are composed of board members typically appointed by state or local officials. Those officials can therefore influence transit decisions through their appointments to the transit authority. Federal money for urban transit tends to go to a state or state department of transportation, which is identified as a special transportation district, but for some systems the city or the transit authority is the direct recipient of federal

11. The Federal Transit Administration (2010) estimated that it would cost $78 billion to bring all U.S. rail and bus transit assets in urban and rural areas to a state of good repair.

12. O'Toole (2006) points out that the U.S. Department of Transportation is structured by systems, such as mass transit, instead of functions, such as urban transportation. Thus, the transportation agencies themselves effectively become lobbyists for the state and local agencies they fund, so they have no interest in a process that might decrease their budget and increase a sister agency's budget.

funds. Obviously, the recipient of federal funds significantly influences how those funds are spent.

Because of the Federal Transit Administration's New Starts program, which helps support transit capital investments, cities have been able to construct new transit systems, especially rail transit, for more than thirty years. Public funds from all levels of government have been invested in twenty-two new light rail systems and five new heavy rail systems. In the future, a greater share of New Starts funding is likely to be spent on bus transit projects because the program is running out of cities that are willing and able to support a (subsidized) rail system.[13] However, the Obama administration has recently announced that it would funnel more money to cities to build streetcars, among other projects, to promote "livability."

Strong support from civic leaders and government for an urban rail system has played a vital role in getting a system built or extended, while opposition from various stakeholders in government can delay a rail project and raise its cost. Following failed efforts in 1982 and 1992, residents of and visitors to Oahu are helping to pay for what is currently estimated to be a $5.3 billion commuter rail system in Honolulu through a 0.5 percent excise tax surcharge. Because the federal government has yet to commit to the project, Oahu may be forced either to raise as much as an additional $1 billion to complete the system or to scale back its coverage. Recently Governor Linda Lingle announced that she is exploring ways to reduce the system's costs because she is concerned that they are putting the state at financial risk.[14] After being planned for more than forty years, the Washington Metro just received the federal government's commitment to partly fund its extension to the Washington Dulles airport and beyond. And it appears that support from private backers will enable Detroit to start building a light-rail system.[15]

An Economic Assessment

Urban transit's subsidies are justified on economic grounds if they are less than the social benefits, including positive externalities, that transit provides. Efficient transit policy should seek to maximize the difference between transit's social benefits and costs, but in practice bus and rail transit policies have

13. "Urban Rail Transit and Freight Railroads: A Study in Contrasts," *Innovation NewsBriefs,* February 18, 2008.

14. Sean Hao and Gordon Y. K. Pang, "Honolulu's Rail Costs Put State at Financial Risk, Governor Says," *Honolulu Advertiser,* January 17, 2010.

15. Mike Scott, "Mass Transit for Motor City," *CNNMoney.com,* February 15, 2010.

created significant inefficiencies that raise questions about whether subsidies for either mode can be justified.

Pricing Inefficiencies

Efficient pricing is crucial for developing an optimal transit network because it identifies the costs and benefits that should enter into the decisions about what routes to serve and how often to serve them. In practice transit pricing has not played that role; instead, its inefficiencies are at the heart of transit's budget deficits. Today more than 80 percent of public transit systems charge a uniform price to all passengers who use the system, regardless of the duration or time of day of a passenger's trip.[16] This pricing policy ignores the higher cost of providing service to riders who travel during peak periods; who travel greater distances; and who travel on low-density routes (thus spreading the costs over fewer passengers than occurs on high-density routes). In addition, uniform transit fares and even fares that vary broadly by time of day and distance are kept well below the short-run marginal cost of transit service to compete with the cost and convenience of automobile travel and to raise total ridership, an important measure considered by policymakers when deciding whether to grant additional subsidies.

Winston and Shirley (1998) find that replacing bus and rail transit fares with fares based on the marginal cost of serving a passenger would, as expected, force travelers to pay higher fares but produce annual social welfare gains of $3 billion (1998 dollars) by reducing public subsidies. As in the case of road pricing, because marginal cost pricing of transit would raise the per-mile cost of public transportation, it would improve land use by causing some households to move closer to their workplaces and increase urban density. However, little quantitative evidence exists on transit's effect on residential location.

Service Inefficiencies

Transit's inefficient operations are indicated by its high share of empty seats, despite its low fares. In the mid-1990s rail filled roughly 18 percent of its seats with paying customers, buses roughly 14 percent. Since then, the Federal Transit Authority has stopped requiring transit systems to report load factor data.[17] Transit's low load factors are attributable to oversized vehicles

---

16. American Public Transit Association, *Public Transportation Fact Book,* various issues.

17. Public transit's average load factor has been declining for some time. It was 22 percent in 1975, 18 percent in 1985, and 16 percent in 1995. The recent weakness in the economy and

on certain routes and at certain times of day, excessive service frequency, and inefficient route coverage.

Urban bus and rail systems tend to use standardized vehicles, instead of a mixed-vehicle fleet that could enable transit managers to adjust seat capacity to variations in passenger demand by time of day and by route.[18] Route frequency and route coverage tend to be determined by transit authorities, but other government officials and certain stakeholders also influence those decisions in a politically charged environment where all taxpayers want access to transit service regardless of whether they use it (Winston and Shirley 1998).

Baum-Snow and Kahn (2005) provide evidence that in those cities where rail systems have not changed their networks, rail's share has declined as former patrons and jobs have moved beyond rail's catchment areas. The same outcome also applies to bus. Winston and Shirley (1998) estimated that setting bus and rail service frequencies to maximize net benefits and charging fares equal to marginal cost reduced transit deficits and frequencies and resulted in an annual welfare gain of $8.9 billion (1998 dollars).[19] Cutting frequencies generates benefits because deficits are reduced by more than the value that urban travelers place on the lost service. In the long run, the social gain would be even greater if transit companies' route coverage and vehicle sizes were adjusted to maximize net benefits.

Production Inefficiencies

Public transit is subject to a host of federal regulations that increase the cost of capital used to provide service. The Federal Transit Administration's "buy American" provisions increase the cost of capital purchases by mandating that mass transit agencies first offer contracts to domestic producers instead of seeking out the most efficient supplier (Hughes 1994). Environmental

---

increases in gasoline prices have undoubtedly caused transit's load factor to increase to some extent. But, as Wendell Cox points out (www.demographia.com/db-hwytr2008f.pdf), only 2.1 percent of the decline in roadway passenger miles during 2008 was captured by public transit. The rest is accounted for by trip chaining and elimination of low-priority trips.

18. In accordance with Federal Transit Administration regulations, a transit agency's total vehicle fleet can exceed the number of vehicles that it uses during the peak period by no more than 20 percent, but a transit agency is not forced by federal regulations to use standardized vehicle sizes. In addition, a variety of bus lengths and rail cars of different sizes are available from manufacturers. However, transit agencies choose to operate with fixed vehicle sizes instead of a mixed fleet, apparently because the latter would complicate scheduling, maintenance practices, and driver utilization. At the same time, agencies could improve load factors and reduce costs by using smaller vehicles on certain routes that do not have pronounced peaking characteristics.

19. Net benefits are composed of travelers' net benefits, bus revenues and costs, and rail revenues and costs.

Protection Agency regulations force transit agencies to ensure that every rebuilt or new bus engine in their fleet conforms to a given pollution standard without cost-benefit considerations.[20] And the agencies themselves seek to customize vehicles for little or no benefit. Because buses are largely purchased through federal grants, transit agencies have little incentive to minimize the cost of the regulations.

Federal regulations also distort investment decisions. Formula grants give transit authorities an incentive to increase system mileage to obtain more capital subsidies, whether or not the additional capacity is socially desirable (Schmidt 2001). And because rolling capital is federally subsidized while maintenance is not, transit agencies are encouraged to replace their capital stock prematurely rather than to maintain it efficiently (Cromwell 1991).

Labor expenses make up two-thirds of urban transit operating costs, with wages accounting for 40 percent and fringe benefits accounting for an additional 26 percent. The high ratio of benefits to wages is attributable to the powerful unions that represent transit workers. Public transit agencies have roughly 358,000 employees, with total annual labor compensation exceeding $20 billion—quantities that have been significantly inflated by federal regulations.[21]

The most costly are labor restrictions within Section 13 (c) of the 1964 Federal Transit Act, which make it extremely expensive to release a transit employee. The act was initially designed to ensure that transit workers would retain labor rights as their sector passed from private to public control during the 1960s. Accordingly, transit agencies receiving federal support must provide any dismissed employee with a monthly compensation package equal to his or her average monthly earnings over the preceding twelve months—with the duration of compensation equal to the employee's length of employment with the transit agency, capped at *six years*. Under those terms and given that the average compensation of a transit worker is approximately $57,000 (the national average for 2006, including wages and benefits), severance packages could approach $350,000 per employee. Thus transit agencies' and local governments' hands are tied if they attempt to reduce their transit labor force in response to changing market conditions or if they want to contract with a private firm to provide transit service. At the

20. The regulations are known as EPA's Retrofit/Rebuild Requirements for 1993 and Earlier Model Year Urban Buses.

21. The figures are from American Public Transit Association, *Public Transportation Fact Book 2008* based on operations in 2006.

same time, some agencies are finding that their payments for overtime work are sharply increasing because track maintenance and vehicle repair must be done on weekends and because as networks expand most train and bus operators do not have runs that fit into neat, eight-hour chunks.[22]

Labor expenses and employment, especially administrative positions, are also increased by regulations that require transit agencies to hold public hearings for any fare or service changes that they wish to make, to complete considerable paperwork to document that they have satisfied "buy American" provisions, and to collect extensive data that in many cases do not appear to be useful.

With ballooning bureaucracies and strong labor protections, it is not surprising that transit labor productivity has sharply declined. In the case of bus transit, Lave (1991) calculated that bus hours per employee fell from 1,228 in 1964 to 1,028 in 1985. If labor productivity had remained constant since 1964, operating costs in 1990 would have been 40 percent lower, and most of the bus transit operating deficit would have been eliminated without raising fares. Large and growing transit deficits further compromise productivity. Karlaftis (2006) surveys the evidence and concludes that increases in transit subsidies encourage inefficiencies to flourish and productivity to decline.

Transit's low productivity also makes it less competitive against the automobile. Winston and Shirley (1998) point out that rail and bus operating costs per seat mile are lower than auto's operating costs per seat mile. But this potential cost advantage is not realized in practice because bus and rail operate with a great deal of excess capacity; hence bus and rail operating costs per *passenger mile* are greater than auto's operating costs per passenger mile. Transit's load factor has recently increased because of greater ridership, but its operating costs have also increased as it tries to accommodate additional passengers and absorb higher energy and steel prices.

Spending Inefficiencies

The efficiency of transit spending, especially for new light and heavy rail systems, and the credibility of public officials who justify building new systems have long been questioned because the costs of building rail systems are notorious for exceeding expectations, while ridership levels tend to be much

22. Lena H. Sun, "Metro Costs for Overtime Are Up 56% since 2002," *Washington Post,* June 5, 2007, reports that overtime costs for the Washington Metro have increased because some drivers, whose regular shifts include being on standby, are paid overtime and because overtime benefits are included in retirees' benefit calculations.

lower than anticipated (Pickrell 1990; Flyvbjerg, Holm, and Buhl 2002).[23] Flyvbjerg, Holm, and Buhl estimate that the average cost escalation for rail projects is roughly 40 percent; thus the extent of the inevitable cost overruns from extending the Washington Metro to Dulles airport and building the new Honolulu rail system should come as no surprise. In fact, periodic media reports on the evolution of those systems indicate that estimates of their final costs have sharply increased.

Cost overruns and spending inefficiencies persist after systems are built. The New York Metropolitan Transit Authority has acknowledged that it may have to postpone or eliminate essential projects less than halfway through its five-year, $21 billion program to expand and improve its transit system because the program is already more than $2 billion over budget.[24] After a heated debate during which the transit authority threatened to raise fares and cut service significantly, the state legislature approved a $2.3 billion bailout for the agency that is largely funded by a payroll tax on wages paid by employers in the counties served by the transit authority and by additional fees on drivers and vehicles. However, the system's long-run financial problems are far from being resolved.

The Government Accountability Office has discovered that some federal employees and nongovernmental workers, who are given subsidies (Metrocheks) that pay for their commutes on the Washington Metro rail and bus system, have defrauded the government of millions of dollars a year by selling the Metrocheks at a discount to buyers who use them to ride the system.[25] As I discuss below, an emerging issue is the social desirability of additional spending on transit given its large inefficiencies.

Finally, in the wake of a tragic crash in June 2009 between Washington Metro trains that killed nine people, rail transit safety programs have come under fire because it was revealed that Metro had failed to purchase a backup system for a possible circuit failure that may have caused the crash. Such a system was bought, for example, by the San Francisco BART system. Metro compounded concerns about its operations by stonewalling requests by

23. It is also possible that certain transit systems have not been built because forecasts of ridership levels and construction costs are too pessimistic. I am not aware of examples where that may have occurred in the United States.

24. William Neuman, "Rising Costs Put N.Y. Transit Projects at Risk," *New York Times*, January 31, 2007.

25. Lyndsey Layton, "GAO Finds Fraud in Commuter Program," *Washington Post*, April 24, 2007. I am not aware that investigations of similar fraud have been made for TransitChek programs in New York City and San Francisco.

independent monitors to inspect its safety procedures. The Obama admin-istration has recently indicated its intention to pass legislation that would allow the federal government to set and enforce safety standards on the nation's subway and light-rail systems.

Technological and Other Innovations

Urban transit has failed to take prompt advantage of recent technological innovations and to explore operating innovations that could improve its ser-vice and financial performance. Many of the innovations have been imple-mented in transit systems overseas. Public transit authorities have limited interest in drawing from their own budgets to develop technological innova-tions because any future cost savings will only decrease the subsidies they receive from the government. Much of the research and development in the transit sector is being carried out by private firms that either market their products directly to riders or sell their innovations to public agencies for a profit. For example, NextBus offers satellite-provided bus location informa-tion to commuters who are online or use a personal digital assistant. Partici-pating transit agencies pay the company to outfit their fleet with the NextBus technology to attract new riders who value the online information. However, in an ironic twist the transit authority did not expect, greater NextBus use in the San Francisco Bay Area is providing hard evidence that Muni bus service is unreliable.[26]

As in the case of highways, emerging transit technologies are in the field of telematics. For example, buses equipped with Global Positioning System (GPS) equipment may improve service times and reliability by using traffic information that is relayed instantly via satellite. The satellite keeps track of each bus in the fleet and ascertains delays for various routes based on cur-rent congestion. A central dispatcher then informs bus drivers of alternative routes that are likely to be faster but still enable passengers to get off at their regular stops.[27] In the future, telematics could facilitate bus and rail service that responds to real-time demand as well as driverless buses and trains that are controlled remotely from a central node.

Urban transit could also improve its operations by making changes that are not on the technological frontier. The most important involves using

---

26. Geoffrey A. Fowler," Transit Riders Hail the New Killer App," *Wall Street Journal*, April 22, 2010.

27. The Montgomery County, Maryland, transportation department has equipped its buses with GPS technology and established a central dispatch center.

minibuses on low-density routes, perhaps as part of a feeder service to urban rail or buses serving high-density routes and during off-peak periods. Currently minibuses account for a tiny fraction of seat miles provided by U.S. bus transit because regulations prevent them from operating in certain major cities such as New York; but with a capacity of fifteen to forty passengers, their operating costs are considerably lower than the operating costs of standard buses, which typically have the capacity to seat seventy passengers (Gomez-Ibanez and Meyer 1998). Transit agencies could make more efficient use of standard buses and increase revenue in off-peak periods by helping to transport primary and secondary school students to and from school and by providing charter service. They could also explore the possibility of providing profitable paratransit and jitney service—the former provides flexible service that does not follow fixed routes or schedules and is typically performed by minibuses. Unfortunately, current regulations prevent most transit systems from using their buses or other vehicles for those (nonscheduled) services.[28]

Generally, an efficient urban transportation system should embody bus and rail transit's comparative advantage when competing with each other and with auto and should exploit the most efficient aspects of a transit operation, such as the low feeder and distribution costs of jitneys and vans in low-density areas, the low line-haul costs of bus in high-density areas, and rail's economies of vehicle size and distance for long-haul trips in very high-density areas.

Summary and Conclusions

Transit's large and growing deficits reflect a myriad of inefficient policies, which, as itemized in table 4-1, reduce revenues and increase costs; some of these policies also help explain why transit's share of urban travelers has declined for several decades. The large deficits and low ridership that have resulted from inefficient operations have reached a point where transit's social desirability is in question. Accounting for possible externalities, Winston and Shirley (1998) found that bus transit's total subsidies exceeded its

---

28. Some bus and rail transit systems transport students on their existing routes. William Neuman, "In Hard Times, Profit at Rochester Transit System," *New York Times*, September 15, 2008, points out that Rochester's Regional Transit Service was able to negotiate additional revenue from the Rochester City School District to cover the costs of serving nearly all of its students in seventh through twelfth grades. In contrast, the New York City rail and bus system provides millions of rides a year to students using free or half-fare passes, and it receives funds from the city and the state that cover only half of the value of the lost fares.

Table 4-1. *Sources of Transit Budget Deficits*

Revenues
- Transit prices are kept well below marginal costs
- Certain commuters are provided with transit services at no charge
- Route coverage does not keep up with demographic changes
- Up-to-date technology is not used to improve service and attract riders
- Transit systems are prevented from providing other services that would raise revenue

Costs
- Regulations raise the cost of transit capital and labor
- Standardized transit vehicle sizes contribute to excess capacity
- Frequency is suboptimal
- Costs are underestimated at various stages of a transit system's evolution

---

Source: Author.

total benefits to urban travelers, and Winston and Maheshri (2007) found that with the exception of BART in the San Francisco Bay Area, the subsidies for each U.S. urban rail system exceed the benefits that each system provides to travelers.

Certainly one must question the social desirability of the New York transit system if the state legislature was compelled to place the burden of the system's bailout on the working public—only a portion of whom use transit or benefit from reduced auto congestion—instead of letting the city transit authority take responsibility for covering the short-run deficit by raising fares for the system's users.[29] Cross-subsidies to poor individuals to help improve their quality of life are generally not opposed, but it is troubling when individuals with average or above-average incomes (the average household income of rail commuters is $85,100 and the average household income of bus commuters is $42,550) are heavily subsidized instead of being asked to assume greater responsibility for financing a publicly provided service that they value.[30]

One must also question the wisdom of the Obama administration for wanting to funnel more money to streetcars. The administration's apparent

29. The city transit authority raised the system's base fare only 25 cents. The bailout temporarily postponed the system's budget problems, which are likely to loom larger as its debt and labor costs continue to grow.

30. Average household incomes of bus and rail commuters are from the Bureau of Transportation Statistics, *National Household Travel Survey* (2001), U.S. Department of Transportation, and expressed in 2008 dollars.

justification—to promote "livability"—could be interpreted as trying to reduce driving and the automobile's externalities, but the justification ignores that streetcars are characterized by limited mobility and high operating costs, which means that they will not attract many motorists and will require large subsidies.

Transit does enhance social welfare in some cases by generating positive externalities—for example, urban rail transit reduces road users' congestion costs (Winston and Langer 2006). But transit also generates negative externalities—for example, bus transit, especially where it operates on bus-only lanes, increases road users' congestion costs (Winston and Langer 2006)—and major transit extensions could, in theory, contribute to sprawl.

Quite often transit operations are also not associated with positive external effects. To take one example, promoters of transit assert that "transit-oriented development"—that is, developing real estate in close proximity to transit, especially rail stations—is a promising means of catalyzing local economic development and raising property values. But case studies have yet to show that after their construction, transit systems have an economically significant effect on employment or land use close to stations or that such benefits greatly exceed the benefits from commercial development that would have occurred elsewhere in the absence of rail construction (Bollinger and Ihlanfeldt 1997; Charles 2001).[31] Recently Levinson (2010) reported that urban rail transit was associated with gains in land values near some stations and with losses because of noise and vibrations along the lines between stations, but he did not make an overall assessment. Winston and Shirley (1998) indicate that any positive externalities from public transit attributable to fewer accidents, less pollution, and reductions in fuel consumption are, at best, likely to be small.

It is important to recognize that recent developments may affect the preceding findings on transit's social desirability. The introduction and growth of additional subsidies, such as those associated with Metrocheks, indicate

31. Lisa Rein and Lena H. Sun, in "Metro Faulted for Failing to Foster Growth at Rail Stations," *Washington Post*, September 2, 2007, point out that the Washington Metro has been ineffective in encouraging either residential or commercial development near stations, which would attract more riders, increase system revenues, and stimulate growth in the surrounding area. Thaddeus Herrick, in "Why Some Cities Think Developing at Rail Stops Is a Mighty Good Road," *Wall Street Journal*, December 6, 2006, identifies certain light-rail systems that could potentially promote development near stations, but he points to Houston as an example where developers have not rushed to build on land that is close to the light-rail corridor.

that actual deficits are considerably greater than those that are reported.[32] In addition, recent changes in the economy that have resulted in a short upward spurt in transit ridership have increased system revenues but also have increased system costs and reduced current sources of public subsidies. The net effect of those developments on transit's social desirability—including how additional subsidies are raised—is not clear.[33]

In any case, social desirability is hardly a demanding standard for a public enterprise to meet. Indeed, it is rare to find one whose social desirability is in question. The fact that transit's performance is questionable even on those grounds is indicative of the extent that urban bus and rail services have been mismanaged in the public sector and been compromised by public policy. Accordingly, the important policy question surrounding recent assessments of transit's social desirability is not whether those systems should be completely abandoned or given additional subsidies but, as I discuss later, whether the private sector could sufficiently improve bus and rail transit's performance, thereby eliminating (or significantly reducing) public subsidies and enabling transit to make a greater contribution to urban mobility.

32. Riders who receive a Metrochek are given a "debit card" that contains their monthly transit subsidy for commuting. When a debit card is used to access bus or rail, the transit system records the patronage as additional revenue. But this amount should be deducted from revenues because it is provided by the government, or more accurately by the taxpayers, and it should be counted as an additional subsidy.

33. The recent developments have not been taken into account in assessments (such as by Nelson and others 2007) of the social desirability of a specific transit system. Transit systems are receiving some funds from the stimulus package. However, such funds are intended to create jobs, not to reduce deficits. If transit capacity is constrained, as some systems have indicated, then the additional funds are likely to be used inefficiently.

5

Airports and Air Traffic Control

The first commercial plane flight in the United States, an eighteen-mile run of the St. Petersburg-Tampa Airboat Line that carried one paying passenger, took place in 1914. Federal Aviation Administration (FAA) domestic forecasts indicate that by 2014 annual airline passenger enplanements will reach roughly 1 billion.[1]

Efficient, technologically up-to-date aviation infrastructure—airports and air traffic control—is essential for moving air travelers safely and quickly from their origins to their destinations. Responsibility for basic aeronautical services in the United States—including terminals, gates, taxiing areas, and runways—lies with local governments that operate airports either directly, as in the case of small airports, or through airport authorities, as in the case of many medium and large airports. The federal Transportation Security Administration (TSA) is responsible for airport security, and the FAA provides air traffic control. In 2004 FAA's air traffic control function was reorganized into the Air Traffic Organization (ATO), a "performance-based" organization that, in contrast to a "rules-based" organization, focuses on serving its customers instead of on following detailed procedures. Nonetheless, the ATO remains an agency within a civil aviation administration that is funded by annual budget appropriations from Congress.

How has aviation infrastructure performed? As shown in figure 5-1, the chance of a passenger dying in a commercial airline accident has steadily declined since air travel began and has become very small during the past few decades. Of course, airlines have a strong financial incentive to maintain safe operations, so it is not clear whether market forces or public infrastructure

1. This chapter draws on and extends Morrison and Winston (2008a).

Figure 5-1. *Passenger Fatalities per Million Aircraft Miles*

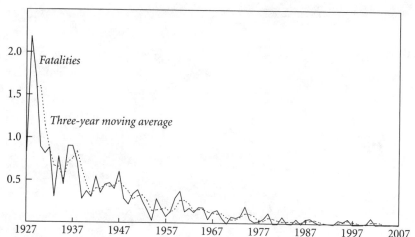

Source: Air Transport Association.
Note: All data reflect systemwide scheduled service performed by U.S. air carriers, including major and commuter carriers, of both passenger and cargo flights operating under 14 CFR Part 121 of Air Carrier Certification. Fatalities include passengers and crew members, but not persons on the ground.

spending and regulations deserve most of the credit for the safety of air travel in the United States.

During the past decade, air travelers have become increasingly concerned about delays they may encounter when going through airport security, leaving the departure gate and taking off, flying to their destination, and landing and disembarking from the aircraft. In-flight delays and earlier airport arrivals for security screening were estimated to cost passengers and airlines in the United States at least $40 billion in 2005.[2] As shown in figure 5-2, travel times

2. Total delay costs for 2005 are obtained as follows. The U.S. Department of Transportation (2006) estimated that aircraft delays cost passengers $9.4 billion. This figure is likely to be an underestimate because the delays to passengers are inferred from delays to aircraft. Passenger delays are likely to be greater than aircraft delays because delays to passengers may cause them to miss connections. The figure also does not include baggage handling delays. Using Federal Aviation Administration delay data, the Air Transport Association in 2006 estimated that the additional operating costs to airlines from delays were $5.9 billion. Finally, a one-hour earlier arrival at an airport for security purposes valued at $50 an hour (obtained by applying Transportation Department guidelines to determine the value of time in 2005 for airline travelers) for roughly 500 million trips resulted in an additional cost to passengers of $25 billion. This figure does not include the loss to airlines from the reduction in passenger volume at airports that is attributable to passenger and baggage screening.

Figure 5-2. *Air Travel Delays*

Change in flight time (minutes)

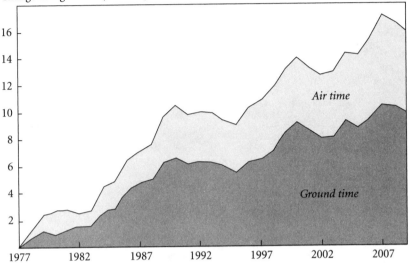

Source: U.S. Department of Transportation, Service Segment Data and Schedule T-100, Data Bank 28DS, Domestic Segment Data. Data for 2009 are through October.

have been increasing for the past three decades. But the problem is becoming so severe that at least one major airline carrier, Air Canada, is offering delay insurance, which pays for lodging and even airfare on rival carriers in the event that it cancels a flight or a traveler misses a connection because of its actions.[3]

In my view, excessive travel delays are—to a significant extent—a manifestation of the failure of publicly owned and managed airports and air traffic control to adopt policies and introduce innovations that could greatly improve the efficiency of the U.S. air transportation system. Given little economic incentive and saddled with institutional and political constraints, major airports and the air traffic control system have not exhibited any marked improvement in their performance for decades despite repeated assurances that they would do so, and they have provided little reason for policymakers and travelers to expect such improvements to ever occur.

3. Scott McCartney, "Letting Fliers Buy Protection against Delays," *Wall Street Journal*, May 20, 2008.

Some observers believe that delays would be reduced if the nation invested more money in building new airports and in upgrading air traffic control technology. Such spending could be economically justified, but its returns would be compromised by the system's vast inefficiencies. Delays should be reduced primarily by efficient pricing of and investment in aviation infrastructure.

Overview of U.S. Aviation Infrastructure and Current Policy

When air travel began in this country, airports were privately owned, often by airlines. Smaller airports continue to be privately owned, but the FAA prohibits private airports from offering commercial service because it may adversely affect the national aviation system. The prohibition is lifted only for those airports that have been approved to participate in a very limited number of privatization experiments that I note in a later chapter.

For the most part, the federal government has shaped the development of aviation infrastructure through congressional funding of—and the FAA's allocation of those funds for—airports and air traffic control. The federal government also has a major presence at airports through the TSA's screening of passengers and luggage. Different regulations and funding sources govern the operations of those services, so it is useful to discuss the evolution of current policy toward them separately.

Airports

The Civil Aeronautics Act of 1938 is notable for instituting economic regulation of fares, entry, and exit in the U.S. airline industry, but it also paved the way for federal funding of airports by authorizing funds to build additional airfields.[4] Previously, states and local governments had sole responsibility for airport planning and issued general obligation bonds that were supported by taxes to pay for runways, terminal construction, and improvements in those facilities. The Federal Airport Act of 1946 created an intergovernmental grant program, providing federal matching funds to states and local governments for airport projects. The program lasted until 1970 when it was replaced by the Airport Development Program, which increased federal funding for construction and improvements at large pubic airports. Since the passage of the Airport and Airway Improvement Act of 1982, federal funding for airport

---

4. Dilger (2003) provides a complete discussion of the major federal legislation related to airports and air traffic control.

projects that seek to enhance airport safety, capacity, security, and the environment are provided under the Airport Improvement Program (AIP). AIP funds are drawn from the Airport and Airway Trust Fund, consisting of revenues from aviation excise taxes, fuel taxes, and other sources, and distributed by the FAA to airports of all sizes on the basis of congressional priorities.[5]

As shown later, the majority of AIP funds are allocated to airports that account for a small share of commercial enplanements. In addition, because the demand for AIP funds exceeds availability, the FAA typically apportions the funds into major entitlement categories such as primary, cargo, and general aviation. Any remaining funds are then distributed at the discretion of the FAA.

Airports continue to issue bonds to help pay for terminals and runways, and they use the passenger facility charge to cover some bond payments for projects approved by the FAA.[6] Airports also meet expenses with revenues generated from parking fees, retail store rents, and advertising display charges. Finally, airports raise revenues by renting terminal facilities such as counters and gates to airlines and by charging landing fees based on an aircraft's weight subject to guidelines set by the FAA. Runway landing fees vary widely, but currently a typical fee is $2.00 per 1,000 pounds of weight. For example, landing fees for a Boeing 757-200 aircraft, with a maximum design landing weight of 198,000 pounds and a capacity of about 186 passengers, would be somewhat less than $3 a passenger for typical passenger loads. During the 1950s and 1960s, as a quid pro quo for airlines agreeing to pay off billions of dollars in airport bonds for expansion projects, airlines obtained exclusive-use gate leases (that is, gates leased exclusively to one airline) at many large and midsize airports.

Airports and airlines use either a residual or a compensatory charging system to establish rents and landing fees (Graham 2004). Passenger facility charges are localized and spent at the airport's discretion. Under a residual charging system, airlines pay the remaining costs of running the airport after commercial and nonairline sources of revenue are taken into account.

5. Currently, the trust fund is composed of revenue from a 7.5 percent ticket tax plus a fee of $3.30 per passenger for each flight segment flown, a fee of $14.50 per passenger for each international departure and arrival, a 6.25 percent cargo waybill tax, a 7.5 percent frequent flier tax on third parties (such as credit card companies) that sell frequent flier miles, and a fuel tax of 4.3 cents a gallon. At the end of fiscal year 2008 the trust fund's uncommitted balance was $1.4 billion—well below its uncommitted balance of $7.3 billion in 2001—and it was expected to fall further in the following years, possibly even to run out.

6. Congress is currently considering legislation that would increase passenger facility charges from $4.50 to $7 a passenger to generate an additional $1.1 billion in revenue for airports.

The airlines guarantee that the level of charges and rents will enable the airport to break even. Under a compensatory charging system, the airlines agree to pay charges that allow the airport to recover the costs of the facilities that the airlines occupy and use. The airport is responsible for covering the remaining costs such as parking and concessions. In practice negotiations between airlines and large and midsize airports have not resulted in a clear preference for one system over the other. In addition airport operations do not appear to be affected by the choice of charging system. Some of the contracts detailing the charges airlines pay to airports contain "majority in interest" clauses that give the airlines signing long-term lease agreements the right to approve certain capital expenditures, especially spending on terminals and gates.

Given a variety of funding sources, airports—in contrast to airlines—have generally been able to maintain their financial health even in the period after September 11, 2001, and in subsequent periods characterized by sky-rocketing fuel bills and a deep recession. To maintain their airline tenants' operations, some airports (among them, Boston, Detroit, Philadelphia, San Francisco, and San Jose) have directly cut fees and charges or offered discounts to carriers that serve additional cities or expand existing service—or taken both steps.

More than 19,000 public and private airports operate in the United States, some 3,300 of which have been identified by the FAA's National Plan of Integrated Airport Systems as significant to national air transportation and therefore eligible to receive federal grants under the AIP. Table 5-1 classifies those airports by size and presents their share of commercial enplanements and federal grants, which are assessed later in the chapter along with other data on the allocation of AIP funds. The thirty-one large hub airports account for more than two-thirds of commercial air travelers, but only one new large hub airport has been constructed since 1973. Built in Denver in 1995, that airport has advantages that are difficult to replicate elsewhere—a flat, largely uninhabited site that is fewer than thirty miles from downtown. More than half of the nation's large hub airports are on sites that were chosen in the 1920s, 1930s, or 1940s and were later significantly expanded (Altshuler and Luberoff 2003). Those airports and others built more recently have expanded available aircraft capacity by building new runways, but adding capacity in this fashion takes considerable time because airports must account for communities' input, especially their opposition to proposed projects. Since 1970 such projects also must satisfy Environmental Protection Agency environmental impact standards.

Table 5-1. *Distribution of Federal Airport Grants, by Airport Size, 2000*

Airport type[a]	Number of airports	Share of grants (percent)	Share of scheduled commercial enplanements (percent)
Large hub	31	24	70
Medium hub	35	15	19
Small hub	71	15	8
Nonhub	282	19	3
General aviation, relievers, and other commercial service	2,981	28	0

Source: U.S. General Accounting Office (2002), Federal Aviation Administration (2000).

a. A large hub handles at least 1 percent of national enplanements, a medium hub from 0.25 percent to 1.0 percent of enplanements, a small hub from 0.05 to 0.25 percent of enplanements. A nonhub has more than 10,000 annual enplanements but less than 0.05 percent of the national total. General aviation, reliever, and other commercial service airports do not provide regularly scheduled commercial flights, although some house air taxi services.

Airport Security

Before the September 11, 2001, terrorist attacks, airlines were responsible for providing passenger screening, and the FAA was responsible for promulgating performance and training standards. The airlines hired roughly 19,500 screeners from private security companies to perform screening procedures at U.S. airports (GAO 2005a).

After the attacks, some observers claimed that reliance on private screeners was disastrous, but it should be noted that the screeners were subject to government regulations. In addition, it is fair to say that the public got what it perceived to be the level of safety that it wanted. In any case, the Transportation Security Administration was initially created as part of the Department of Transportation and in February 2002 it assumed responsibility for screening at virtually all U.S. airports; in November 2002 it was folded into the newly created Department of Homeland Security. By the end of 2002 the TSA deployed a workforce that, accounting for temporary employees, had grown to more than 50,000 screeners.

Passengers pay $2.50 for each leg of their flight, up to a maximum of $10 a round trip, to help pay for security screening. Airlines then remit the fees to the TSA to help support its annual budget of roughly $5.5 billion.[7] To

7. The fiscal year 2011 budget proposal for the Department of Homeland Security includes a $1 increase in each passenger's security fee.

facilitate flexibility in staffing that can respond to changes in airline service, airports have been given the option to replace federal screeners with screeners from private companies. But private screeners are still overseen by federal employees and are required to be paid at least as much as federal ones and to have undergone the same training. Not surprisingly, only a handful of (small) airports have applied to the government to use privately employed screeners.

In response to air travelers' complaints about the excessive delays created by TSA screening at major airports, a "registered traveler" program was initiated to create special, speedier airport security lines for people who are willing to pay an annual fee of $50 to $100 and undergo background checks. However, the TSA has balked at Congress's direction to conduct background checks on registered traveler applicants and to provide expedited screening to those who passed. That undercut the potential value that the three approved registered traveler companies offered to members, and caused Clear, the largest provider, to enter bankruptcy. Its new owners and another entrant have announced their intention to relaunch security-screening lanes by the fall of 2010. Airlines, such as American and United, have tried to expedite screening at certain airports by instituting special security lines for travelers who are elite members of their frequent flier programs.

Air Traffic Control

The scope of federal provision of air traffic control was expanded by a series of fatal midair collisions and thousands of near misses during the mid-1950s. Concerned that the negative publicity about air safety would sharply curtail passenger demand, aviation interests supported the creation of a larger federal agency to oversee air traffic control and other safety issues. Thus, in an atmosphere of crisis, Congress passed the Federal Aviation Act of 1958, which gave enhanced responsibility for managing the nation's navigable airspace to the new Federal Aviation Agency (renamed the Federal Aviation Administration in 1967, when it was brought into the newly established Department of Transportation, or DOT).

In practice the FAA operates facilities to ensure that air travel is safe and to prevent the system from becoming congested both along the flight route and near airport terminals. En route facilities include air route traffic control centers (ARTCCs) that provide air traffic control service to aircraft operating under instrument flight rules within controlled airspace.[8] Terminal facilities include radar towers at airports and terminal radar approach facilities (TRACONs) within a fifty-mile radius of an airport; both provide service to

8. ARTCCs may also assist with aircraft flying under visual flight rules.

aircraft that are arriving, departing, and transiting the controlled airspace. The FAA system includes roughly one hundred and fifty radar towers, thirty-five TRACONs, and twenty-one ARTCCs. The FAA is also responsible for hiring air traffic controllers and other air traffic control personnel and for supplying terminal and en route facilities with new equipment.

The FAA and its programs are supported by the Airport and Airway Trust Fund as well as by general revenues. Commercial airlines pay for more than 90 percent of the costs of the system, while private business jets pay for most of the small remaining share. In addition, the military provides as well as uses air traffic control. Given that commercial airlines account for only two-thirds of all flights, they contend that they are overpaying for air traffic control services.

The FAA funds research and development to improve air travel safety and efficiency, but an ongoing challenge for the agency has been to adopt and implement the latest technological advances to expand the airspace where planes can fly safely and to reduce controller error and aircraft encounters with dangerous weather, both of which contribute to accidents. For example, during the early 1980s the FAA announced plans to develop an advanced automation system to provide flexible, computer-oriented air traffic control capable of handling greater traffic volumes at reduced manpower. The system also included significant improvements in detecting wind shear, the primary cause of several crashes, including two major ones in the 1980s.

Although some progress has certainly been made in implementing that system, its development has been characterized by delays and inefficiencies.[9] Scheduled to be completed by 1991 for $12 billion, the fully upgraded system is almost two decades late, billions of dollars over budget, and still nowhere in sight. As of 2007 the cost of the modernization was expected to climb to $51 billion (current dollars).

Moreover, by the time the FAA's upgrade is complete, the system will be approaching technological obsolescence. Air travel can become even safer and faster if air traffic control replaces its ground-based radar systems with more accurate and reliable satellite communications. The satellite-based system, known as NextGen (for Next Generation) would allow pilots and controllers to be cognizant of other planes in the vicinity as well as their speeds, headings, and flight numbers. Travel times would be reduced because planes

---

9. The U.S. General Accounting Office issued a series of reports in the late 1990s that critically assessed the FAA's progress in modernizing the air traffic control system (GAO 1998, 1999a, 1999b). More recent critical assessments include Dillingham (2003) and Mead (2003).

would be able to fly closer together and take the most direct routes to their destinations using signals from global position satellites to navigate. In addition, NextGen would provide real-time information about wind conditions to facilitate optimal altitudes and routings, save fuel, and increase throughput. Finally, pilots would be able to operate in cloudy and foggy weather much as they do on clear days. Radar is imprecise—it typically updates aircraft positions every 4.8 seconds and forces controllers to separate aircraft by several miles to avoid collisions. In contrast, the automatic dependent surveillance broadcast (a key component of NextGen known by the acronym ADS-B) updates positions every second. The FAA has recently proposed a rule for airlines and business jets to equip all aircraft operating in controlled airspace with ADS-B-compatible avionics by 2020.

NextGen could also increase throughput at airports by making it feasible to provide short-haul service on 3,000 foot runways because certain aircraft types (such as planes carrying no more than 100 passengers) would be able to follow precise independent approach and departure paths in a metropolitan area's terminal airspace. Such aircraft could use underutilized short runways at major hubs and serve reliever airports in the same metropolitan area as a congested hub airport.

Because the NextGen system would require only a few dozen facilities dispersed throughout the country, managing that system would be much simpler and less costly than managing the current system. Much of the current system of radar towers, TRACONS, and en route centers would be eliminated. The remaining facilities would be consolidated, with some providing backup capabilities in case of a major system failure. By replacing most radars with ADS-B equipment on planes, along with ground-based equipment, thousands of costly-to-maintain radars and other ground-based navigation aids could be retired.

Key components of the system are moving forward, after having been tested in Alaska. Although Alaska is not representative of most flying conditions, the FAA reports that since ADS-B satellite navigation was first deployed in aircraft, the fatality rate for general aviation in Alaska has dropped roughly 40 percent.[10] The system's technology is also being used for commercial airline flights across the Gulf of Mexico, by helicopters serving Gulf oil platforms, by UPS at its air cargo hub in Louisville, Kentucky, and by Alaska Airlines for flights into and out of Seattle airport. US Airways will engage

10. Del Quentin Wilber, "Overhaul of Air Traffic System Nears Key Step," *Washington Post,* August 27, 2007.

in a trial in 2010 in the Northeast corridor airspace, when part of its fleet is equipped with ADS-B. Southwest Airlines is the first airline to commit to upgrading its entire fleet to use satellite-based navigation approaches to airports. The FAA plans to switch completely from today's radar-based to satellite-based air traffic control—that is, to replace the system it has been working on for more than twenty years but has not fully completed. However, the timetable, as outlined by the Joint Planning and Developing Office that is coordinating the effort, calls for NextGen to take twenty-five years to complete at a cost of at least $30 billion.[11]

In sum, the federal government has shaped the nation's aviation infrastructure through its long-term strategic planning and design, allocation of funds, project approval process, and specific policy guidelines on runway charges, air traffic control charges, and the like. I now consider how the government's pervasive presence has affected the air transportation system's performance.

An Economic Assessment

The value that travelers place on air transportation reflects its convenience, price, and safety. In theory, aviation infrastructure policy should enhance those attributes by efficiently reducing travel delays, facilitating greater airline competition, and using the most effective technology to keep flying safe. In practice, the evidence indicates that current policy should be reformed to make greater progress toward achieving all of those goals.

Performance of Airports

Airport policy encompasses charging aircraft for their use of the runways, investing in runways, leasing gates, and screening passengers and luggage. I draw on scholarly and anecdotal evidence to assess the efficiency of current policies.

RUNWAY PRICING. As noted, airports charge airlines landing fees that are based on the weight of the aircraft and that are consistent with the terms of the residual or compensatory contract that the parties negotiate. Generally,

11. Jennifer Oldham, "Nation's Air Traffic Control Again Nearing Obsolescence," *Los Angeles Times,* June 3, 2006; Barbara Peterson, "End of Flight Delays?" *Popular Mechanics,* August 2007. In fact, the $30 billion figure may seriously underestimate the cost of NextGen. As reported by the Associated Press, "Air Traffic Upgrade Costs Seen Ballooning," February 7, 2008, Calvin L. Scovel III, inspector general for the U.S. Department of Transportation, indicated that the system's software development alone could cost more than $50 billion.

the fees do not vary by time of day. But congestion—which delays travelers—does, in accordance with the volume of aircraft traffic. Beginning with Levine (1969) and Carlin and Park (1970), researchers have called for airports to reduce delays by replacing weight-based landing fees with efficient landing and takeoff tolls based on an aircraft's contribution to congestion.

Weight-based landing fees were probably a reasonable way to allocate airport costs and raise revenue when airports were not severely congested, but today the principal cost that an aircraft imposes when it takes off or lands is the delay it imposes on other aircraft. (Runway damage caused by most aircraft is small.) Based on a sample of aircraft operations at thirty-one of the most congested airports in the United States, Morrison and Winston (1989) found that this delay can be substantial. For example, the elasticity of average departure delay, defined as the percentage change in average departure delay caused by a 1 percent change in aircraft departures, is 2.9 for commercial carriers and 2.5 for general aviation. Thus, current weight-based landing fees, which charge large planes much more than they charge small planes but account for a small share of large planes' operating costs, have little effect on congestion because a plane waiting to take off or land is delayed at least the same amount of time by a small private plane as by a jumbo jet.[12]

Morrison and Winston modeled airport users' demand and the relationship between airport operations and delay and estimated that replacing weight-based landing fees with efficient marginal-cost takeoff and landing tolls could generate significant annual net benefits to the nation. Travelers would reap $5.3 billion in reduced delay costs, and carriers would gain $1.8 billion from lower operating costs. And although airports would gain substantial revenue from higher takeoff and landing fees, that gain would be modestly exceeded by travelers' losses in consumer surplus as airlines pass on the cost of the tolls in higher ticket prices. That difference would partly offset the gains to travelers and carriers, resulting in net benefits of nearly $6 billion (expressed in 2005 dollars). As discussed below, the redistribution from travelers to airports would be softened if efficient tolls were combined with efficient runway investment.

12. To be more precise, delay is affected by the type of lead and trailing aircraft (Ball, Donohue, and Hoffman 2006). If the lead aircraft is small, then the flight separation time for a heavy aircraft (that is, one with a maximum certified takeoff weight of 300,000 pounds or more) is 64 seconds and the flight separation time for a small aircraft is 80 seconds. Those times are comparable. But if the lead aircraft is heavy, then the flight separation time for a small aircraft, 240 seconds, is much greater than the flight separation time for a heavy aircraft, 100 seconds.

Recently Brueckner (2002) raised doubts about the extent to which optimal airport pricing would reduce delays. In the case of highway travel, efficient tolls charge motorists for the delay they cause all motorists. But in the case of air travel, a given American Airlines flight, for example, may delay another American Airlines flight. It could be argued that American Airlines' operations take that delay into account, or "internalize" the delay.[13] Thus, American should be charged only for the delays it imposes on other carriers. If American has a 50 percent share of operations at an airport, it should be charged for one-half of the delay costs it creates—the delay imposed on other carriers—whereas the carrier's smaller (atomistic) competitors with a very small share of airport operations should be charged for all the delay they create because their delay is imposed virtually entirely on other carriers. Mayer and Sinai (2003) apply this idea to hub airports where dominant carriers cluster their operations to provide convenient connections for passengers (while nondominant carriers operate most of their flights at less congested times); thus, optimal tolls at hub airports should be small because most delay at hub airports is internalized.

Of course, the fully efficient charges at congested airports would raise political problems because carriers with smaller market shares would pay higher charges than carriers with larger market shares would pay, or they may be forced to abandon the airport. However, those issues appear to be moot because Morrison and Winston (2007) find that the large welfare improvement from setting congestion tolls that assume atomistic behavior would increase only modestly if optimal tolls were set along the lines suggested by Brueckner and by Mayer and Sinai. The reasons are that a large fraction of delays is caused by commercial and commuter carriers and general aviation that behave atomistically (that is, there is more than twice as much external delay as internal delay), and that the nature of carriers' (private) average costs and their (social) marginal costs, the two factors that account for the costs of congestion for a given level of traffic, means that the benefits from correctly charging carriers for contributing to congestion greatly exceed the costs of incorrectly charging them when their congestion has been internalized.

Instead of using the price mechanism at congested airports to curb delays efficiently, the FAA has instituted arbitrary quantity controls, namely, takeoff and landing slots, at some airports. Since 1969 limits—called slots—have been set on the number of takeoffs and landings per hour at New York

---

13. Daniel (1995) empirically explored the extent to which an airline's internalization of delay costs affected its pattern of operations.

LaGuardia, New York Kennedy, Washington Reagan National, and Chicago O'Hare airports. Slots are now also in effect at Newark Liberty Airport. Although it is theoretically possible to design a slot system that has the same welfare properties as efficient tolls, no evidence exists that slot controls at U.S. airports have been designed optimally, whereas evidence does exist that slots have tended to reduce competition and raise fares (Morrison and Winston 2000).[14]

Congress has acted in the past to eliminate slots, but the FAA has countered by imposing administrative controls in response to traffic growth. For example, the FAA has dealt with congestion at O'Hare by getting hub carriers together in a room and allowing American Airlines and United Airlines to agree to reduce flights, and it has proposed a new rule at New York LaGuardia, which was eventually withdrawn, that would discourage the use of small jets by imposing an average plane size of 105 to 122 seats for all gates at the airport. Both actions exemplify the FAA's preference for an (inefficient) administrative solution over a potentially efficient market-oriented solution.

In the summer of 2007 air travel delays—a large fraction of which emanate from the New York area airports—reached record heights and inconvenienced millions of travelers. Under the leadership of then Transportation Secretary Mary Peters and Assistant Secretary Tyler Duvall, the department tried to introduce efficient pricing policies to reduce airport congestion but encountered strong—and ultimately successful—opposition from airlines, airport authorities, and certain members of Congress.

One new federal policy allows airports to charge higher landing fees during peak periods; that change to federal airport rates and charges policy went into effect in 2008 (the federal appeals court recently rejected a challenge by the airline industry to this policy).[15] Secretary Peters' proposal to auction off some takeoff and landing slots at New York Kennedy, LaGuardia, and Newark airports met with even stronger opposition. The airlines preferred to have airports cap the total number of flights during peak hours to reduce congestion—of course, competition would also be reduced and fares increased.

---

14. I am not aware of evidence that slots produce benefits in reduced delays that offset their costs. Whalen and others (2008) suggest that an auction system with well-defined property rights could be used to efficiently allocate slots to air carriers.

15. Levine (2007) points out legal and other issues that have to be addressed to implement airport congestion pricing successfully. These include providing no exemptions for foreign carriers and general aviation, addressing the monopoly airport problem where it exists, and using the revenues from congestion pricing to expand airport capacity but not for other unrelated purposes.

Because policy toward the New York area airports is likely to set the tone for policy toward other congested airports, the dispute between the administration and key stakeholders intensified and the auction proposal was blocked in federal court. The new secretary of transportation, Ray LaHood, cancelled the proposal in May 2009, claiming to still be serious about tackling congestion in the region and planning to seek input from stakeholders about the best ways to move forward. The opposition to the department's laudable efforts under Secretaries Peters and Duvall is indicative of the obstacles to trying to implement efficient policies in publicly owned transportation facilities.

RUNWAY INVESTMENT. During the past fifty years, public officials have attempted to keep up with growing demand for air travel primarily by building more runways at existing airports rather than by building additional large airports. Any effort to build new large airports would encounter significant logistical, financial, and political challenges, but even adding a new runway is fraught with hurdles because airports must contend with community opposition and meet federal environmental impact standards. Indeed, the nation's thirty-one large hub airports, which account for the majority of delays, built just three new runways during the 1980s and six during the 1990s. In 1999 the Air Transport Association, representing major air carriers, and the National Air Traffic Controllers joined forces and called for "fifty miles of concrete"—the equivalent of twenty-five new runways—as an antidote to growing delays. More than a dozen runways have been christened since then, but the time and cost to build some of them have been excessive. For example, it took Atlanta nearly twenty-five years and an estimated cost of $1.3 billion to have its new (fifth) runway; Boston's sixth runway was put into service at the end of 2006, thirty years after it was initially planned; and St. Louis's new runway cost $1.1 billion while its value to travelers is questionable because the airport now has excess capacity (partly because TWA's airline assets were acquired by American Airlines). The construction of taxiways has also been delayed. For example, after a seven-year delay, Boston was scheduled to finish construction of a taxiway in 2009 to reduce the danger of plane collisions.

Runway investments often meet opposition when they are part of an airport's comprehensive plan to upgrade its facilities. For example, Los Angeles airport (LAX) has been trying for more than a decade to develop a proposal acceptable to the surrounding residential community and the FAA that would involve building a new terminal and reconfiguring some of its runways. Chicago O'Hare has also been trying for decades to gain approval for an expansion plan that would add two new runways, lengthen and widen some of its existing runways, and build new passenger terminals and parking spaces for oversize jets and passenger jet bridges. The plan was expected to alleviate delays caused by O'Hare's intersecting runways and vulnerability to winds from the southwest. O'Hare finally succeeded in moving ahead with a $15 billion expansion plan; but after overcoming delays, in part because homes had to be demolished and a cemetery had to be moved, the city enraged United Airlines and American Airlines and jeopardized the project by recently announcing that it planned to raise terminal rents and landing fees.[16]

The impediments to building new runways efficiently should be of great concern because their potential benefits are huge. Morrison and Winston (1989) analyzed the situation where an airport owns land and is able to construct an additional runway measuring 10,000 feet by 150 feet. Optimal runway capacity is reached when the marginal cost of an additional runway is equated with the marginal benefit of reduced delay. Morrison and Winston found that a policy of efficient congestion tolls and optimal runway capacity could generate roughly $16 billion (2005 dollars) in annual benefits. Travelers would gain nearly $12 billion in reduced delays and also would pay lower fares because the expansion in runway capacity would reduce congestion to such an extent that, on average, landing fees would fall.[17] Carriers benefit from the lower operating costs from reduced delay, while airports' net revenues would fall slightly. But because airports are characterized by overall constant returns to scale, they would be financially self-sufficient under optimal pricing and investment (Morrison 1983).

To be sure, Morrison and Winston's findings largely neglect the practical and political difficulties that many airports face when trying to expand their runway capacity. That said, airports that have recently opened a new runway are providing very favorable reports—for example, Chicago O'Hare's new runway in 2008 is claimed to have reduced average airport delays from twenty-four minutes to sixteen.[18] In sum, the reductions in delays from additional runways at most major airports are so large and so important in softening the distributional effects of optimal pricing that federal policy

16. Julie Johnsson and John Hilkevitch, "United, American Threaten to Call Off O'Hare Expansion Talks," *Chicago Tribune,* February 10, 2010.

17. General aviation would face higher landing fees. But the Morrison-Winston model does not account for the greater flexibility that people who use general aviation have in their choice of airport and arrival and departure time; thus their loss is overstated.

18. Scott McCartney, "How a New Runway at O'Hare Makes Travel Easier for All," *Wall Street Journal,* July 22, 2009. To be sure, the reported delay savings attributable to a new runway may capture other factors, such as airlines' reductions in flights as a result of lower demand, which affect delays.

has unquestionably compromised traveler and carrier welfare by helping to turn runway construction into a task that is measured in decades and billions of dollars.[19]

Federal grants under the Airport Improvement Program are used to reduce delays at airports; however, the program suffers from two inefficiencies. First, political forces cause federal funds to be distributed more broadly across airports than they would be if they were allocated according to cost-benefit guidelines. In fiscal year 2009 the 100 largest metropolitan airports, which account for 84 percent of airline passengers, received only 37 percent of AIP funds.[20] Given that the nation's large and medium hub airports serve 89 percent of the nation's passengers and receive only 39 percent of federal airport grant dollars, table 5-1 also suggests a modest correlation between the airports that receive federal funds for projects that are primarily intended to reduce travel delays and the airports that experience the greatest delays. It is particularly striking that 28 percent of the grants go to small airports that are likely to process a small number of daily operations and that do not offer commercial service by regularly scheduled carriers.[21] The AIP program has also not been immune to earmarking that has occurred in highway spending. An obvious example is the newly renamed but little-used John Murtha Johnstown-Cambria County Airport, for which the late representative John Murtha of Pennsylvania secured at least $150 million during the past decade.

Second, efficient runway prices signal which airports will benefit most from additional runway investment. But the AIP program does not make decisions using this signal; instead it makes them subject to constraints on efficient runway investments just noted.

GATE UTILIZATION AND AIRPORT ACCESS. Airport gates are classified as exclusive use (leased exclusively to one airline), preferential use (the

19. One federal agency, the Food and Drug Administration, recognized that the delays it imposed on the introduction of new drugs were generating large social costs. Accordingly, as part of the 1992 Prescription Drug User Fee Act, the FDA set user fees that were paid by pharmaceutical companies and used the revenues to hire additional new drug reviewers to improve the speed and efficiency of its reviews. In contrast, although the FAA has recently claimed that it is streamlining environmental reviews (see Benet Wilson, "FAA: Airport Capacity Improved with Boost in Runways Built," *Aviation Now,* September 26, 2006), it is not clear that the FAA has expedited the construction of new runways.

20. The figures are from Brookings Metropolitan Center calculations based on data from the FAA Airport Improvement Program.

21. Chase Davis, "Tiny Iowa Airports Take Off with Millions in FAA Grants," *Des Moines Register,* June 4, 2008, reports that since 2007, 42 percent of Iowa's AIP grants have gone to airports that provide no commercial service and that process fewer than fifty takeoffs and landings a day.

airport operator may assign the gate temporarily to another carrier when it is not being used by the lessee), or common use (the airport authority makes all gate assignments). Gates available for use by new entrants consist of common-use gates, preferential-use gates that are made available by the airport authority, and exclusive-use gates that are made available by incumbent carriers. In a 1998 survey of forty-one major airports, the Air Transport Association found that 56 percent of the gates were exclusive use, 25 percent were preferential use, and 18 percent were common use, resulting in 25 percent of the gates available for use by new entrants (Morrison and Winston 2000, p. 23).

The prevalence of exclusive-use gates that are not made available to other carriers—a legacy of airline-airport contractual arrangements established during the 1950s and 1960s—makes it difficult for new entrants to provide service at several airports. Another problem facing nonincumbent carriers, especially at airports where most gates are exclusively leased, is that they must often sublet gates from incumbent carriers at nonpreferred times and at a higher cost than the incumbent pays.

In principle an airport has a legal obligation to provide reasonable access to the facility. Policymakers, however, have yet to define precisely what *reasonable* means. Hence, some incumbents are able to prevent competitors from having access even to gates that are little used. For example, Delta offers just thirty-nine departures a day at LAX but still uses sixteen gates in two terminals.[22] Since 2002 JetBlue has expressed an interest in serving Chicago O'Hare, but subleasing a gate from another carrier was a difficult proposition because incumbents did not welcome the competition.[23] Finally, in 2006 JetBlue received federal authorization, which was needed because O'Hare is slot constrained, for four daily departures. Virgin America has faced obstacles in developing its U.S. network because it has been unable to serve Newark airport, expand its operations at New York Kennedy airport, or establish service at O'Hare.[24]

In a few cases, airports have actually bought back and terminated long-term leases on their own gates. For example, the Maryland Aviation Administration agreed to pay US Airways $4.3 million to give up twenty-nine gates at Baltimore-Washington airport, enabling expansion by Southwest and

22. Scott McCartney, "Fewer Travelers Routed through 'Hub' Airports," *Wall Street Journal,* February 14, 2006, p. D4.

23. Mark Skertic, " 'Jet Who' Has City Blues," *Chicago Tribune,* January 8, 2006.

24. Susan Stellin, "Seeking a Place at Airports," *New York Times,* January 26, 2010.

AirTran.[25] And the Los Angeles Airport Commission voted to spend up to $154 million to take over several terminals at LAX to free up aircraft parking spots for discount carriers and other airlines that had tried to add flights at the airport.[26]

Morrison and Winston (2000) found that, all else equal, fares are $4.4 billion (2005 dollars) higher annually because of the limited availability of gates at many major and midsize airports. The loss to travelers reflects the competitive disadvantages that new entrants face when they are unable to acquire gates or can acquire them only at nonpreferred times and locations or at excessive cost.[27]

Finally, commercial carriers' access can be delayed and even blocked at existing airports by regulatory proceedings. In 2006 Southwest Airlines proposed to offer flights at Boeing Field in Washington State, but after receiving input from various stakeholders, including policymakers who were concerned about how Southwest's service would affect Alaska Airlines, King County officials blocked the proposal. Horizon Air and Allegiant Air have proposed to fly passengers from Paine Field, located thirty miles north of Seattle. But federal environmental reviews have already delayed commercial service for a few years, and local residents who oppose flights could use the process to delay service even longer. Such examples indicate that commercial air carriers may encounter obstacles to serving private airports even if commercial service is no longer prohibited at those airports.

Performance of Airport Security

An efficient airport security system allocates resources based on costs and benefits by directing expenditures toward detecting the greatest threats to safety and preventing them from materializing. Although I am not aware of a formal economic assessment of the Transportation Security Administration's passenger screening, the Department of Homeland Security, GAO, and the TSA routinely test screeners' ability to intercept weapons smuggled through checkpoints. The results have been poor. Both GAO and Homeland

25. Scott McCartney, "Airports Crack Down on Games," *Wall Street Journal,* June 7, 2005.

26. Jennifer Oldham, "Panel Acts to Control LAX Terminals," *Los Angeles Times,* January 9, 2007.

27. Private entrepreneurs are not precluded by airport authorities from building gates and leasing or selling them to new entrants. But they are subject to the airport authority's determination of what constitutes a fair and reasonable charge for the use of a gate. This regulatory arrangement has apparently dissuaded private entities from building gates at airports where new entrants face difficulties in acquiring them.

Security found that screening was no more effective by April 2005 than before September 11, and in 2006 screeners failed twenty of the TSA's twenty-two tests.[28] GAO (2008) reported that covert tests through June 2007 conducted by the TSA's Office of Inspection (OI) identified vulnerabilities in the commercial aviation system at airports of all sizes. But the TSA apparently lacks a systematic process to ensure that the OI's recommendations are appropriately incorporated to improve airport security.

Current screening procedures are also inefficient. The annual cost of TSA security includes its budget of $5.5 billion, several billions of dollars in time costs incurred by passengers waiting to be screened, and $1.1 billion in lost revenue to airlines from reduced passenger volume at major airports (Blalock, Kadiyali, and Simon 2007). GAO (2009a) reports that the TSA spent more than $800 million on new air passenger screening technology between 2002 and 2008 but has not used any of it.

It is, of course, difficult to assess the benefits of TSA screening because we do not know of any terrorist attacks that screening has prevented. In any case, federal screeners have intercepted some 7 million prohibited items, but only six hundred were firearms while the rest were nail scissors, penknives, and the like.[29] Those findings are consistent with many critics' assessment of the TSA's first-generation passenger and bag screening: it could stop most amateurs but not anyone seriously committed to bringing weapons or some type of explosive onto a plane. In December 2009 a Nigerian man succeeded in bringing explosive chemicals onto a Detroit-bound Northwest Airlines flight only to be foiled in his attempt to blow up the plane by his own incompetence and passengers' actions. Homeland Security Secretary Janet Napolitano said the man was properly screened before getting on the flight to Detroit from Amsterdam.

The recent incident has illustrated the inefficiencies of expending billions of dollars in time and money to confiscate firearms—almost all of which were probably intended for recreational use—and of using Federal Air Marshals. Stewart and Mueller (2008) conclude that it was far more cost-effective to put bulletproof doors on cockpits, which the airline industry did for some $300 million to $500 million.

Moreover, the incident suggests the importance of taking a risk-based approach toward security that would be better targeted toward keeping

28. Becky Akers, "A Better Way than the TSA," *Christian Science Monitor,* March 21, 2007.

29. Anne Applebaum, "Airport Security's Grand Illusion," *Washington Post,* June 15, 2005, p. A25.

dangerous people off airplanes.[30] To that end, greater efforts should be made to classify travelers according to their risk to airline passengers' safety. Lower-risk people would belong to a "trusted traveler" program and even supply fingerprints and other biometric data stored on smart chips to move quickly through security. Higher-risk people would be placed on an expanded list based on background investigations and intelligence work and would be subject to more intensive screening and, if necessary, to a full body search.[31] More rapid introduction of technologically advanced screening technologies would enhance the approach. For example, body-scanning technologies are more effective than metal detectors are at spotting potentially dangerous objects and substances and can do so with minimal radiation exposure. But the TSA has been very slow to introduce full-body scanners and they are just starting to be deployed.

A fundamental concern is whether the TSA should even exist. One alternative that is likely to be superior to the TSA on cost-benefit grounds is a variant of Israel's model, where a branch of law enforcement receives additional funding and is responsible for identifying and questioning suspicious passengers. Initially the enforcement branch could be used at some selected airports, and its responsibilities and funding could be expanded if this strategy was determined to be superior to using the TSA.

Private security firms that are not subject to federal regulations have been able to provide effective and subtle security for millions of customers at high-risk facilities in the United States, such as casinos in Las Vegas and Atlantic City and major amusement parks such as Disney World. Private security firms could be hired at airports, not just to replace federal screeners with private screeners but to develop security strategies and make safety investments to anticipate and respond to potential terrorist attacks—actions that private sector airport screeners did not take before September 11 when they were regulated by the government. Such firms could also be bonded, giving them strong financial incentives to provide effective security, and could interact with government law enforcement agencies as necessary.

It has also been claimed that government bureaucracy has discouraged research and development of new innovative solutions to combat terrorism,

30. Robert Poole, "Are We Going to Get Serious about Aviation Security?" (Los Angeles: Reason Foundation, December 29, 2009).

31. After a review of security at international airports following the attempt to blow up a jetliner bound for Detroit, President Obama approved using an intelligence-based security system to identify passengers who could have links to terrorism; see Jeff Zeleny, "Security Check System for Flights to U.S. to Be Altered," *New York Times*, April 1, 2010.

causing a political disagreement over whether the government or the private sector should drive the development of security technology.[32]

Performance of Air Traffic Control

Today the probability of dying in a commercial aviation crash is at an all-time low, following a dramatic improvement in safety during the past ten years.[33] FAA expenditures on air traffic control deserve some credit for the nation's improved safety record (Morrison and Winston 2008b); but the FAA's inefficient pricing of and investment in the system and its slow adoption of the latest technology have exacerbated air travel delays. In addition some observers in industry and academia caution that air transport safety could be threatened if the air traffic control system is not expeditiously upgraded to handle the expected growth in traffic over the next decade.

PRICING. The relevant consideration in pricing air traffic control services is the marginal cost that a given flight imposes on the air traffic control system, including delay costs to other users. The cost clearly increases with the volume of traffic in a controller's airspace. Because the ticket tax is based on a percentage of the price of a given flight that may or may not vary with the time of day and, incidentally, with air space congestion, it does not force a plane to account for the delays it imposes on other aircraft. In addition, because of the intensity of airline competition, real average fares have declined over time; thus, the ticket tax is not a stable source of revenue.

As air traffic controllers try to manage congested airspace near airports, delays may take the form of slower air speeds, indirect routings, suboptimal altitudes, and the like. Unscheduled aircraft (general aviation) may cause greater delays than scheduled aircraft cause because of unpredictable peaks in their demand for airspace, especially near airports, and because general aviation prefers altitude approach levels that create additional complexity for controllers. Those costs are also not reflected in the ticket tax.

I am not aware of any studies that quantify the welfare effects of replacing current air traffic control charges based on the ticket tax with appropriately measured marginal-cost user fees. The Congressional Budget Office (1992) reports rough estimates of the marginal cost of services provided by air traffic control. But because of data limitations, those estimates are based on the unrealistic assumption that all air traffic control facilities are optimized. Investment

32. Dan Luzadder, "Airports, Tech Firms in Holding Pattern on New Security Systems," *Travel Weekly*, November 8, 2006.

33. In 1997 there was one fatal crash in the United States for every 2 million departures. After ten years of improvement in air safety, that ratio in 2006 was one fatal crash for every 4.5 million departures.

in those facilities, however, has not been optimal. Under efficient (marginal-cost) pricing and investment, air traffic control operations would likely be designed so that they exhaust any scale economies and fully cover costs.

A fundamental problem in determining efficient charges for air traffic control services is that the FAA has had historic difficulties in establishing their costs. In fact, Russell Chew, the former head of the FAA's Air Traffic Organization, which operates the air traffic system, acknowledged that, after extensive work by analysts, "an understanding of air traffic control costs is only now just coming."[34] In any case, I expect the efficiency gains from marginal-cost pricing, as reflected in reduced delay for travelers and lower operating costs for carriers, would be significant given that the ticket tax bears little relationship to the costs that an aircraft imposes on the system and on other aircraft and does little to discourage planes from using airspace near airports during congested periods. In addition, marginal-cost user fees would generate revenues that cover the costs of air traffic control services.

The expiration on September 30, 2007, of the taxes and fees that support the U.S. Airport and Airways Trust Fund and the trust fund's reauthorization provided an opportunity for the FAA and Congress to reconsider how the air traffic control system should be funded. Not surprisingly, input has been provided by the system's users. Commercial airlines support user fees, instead of the ticket tax, because they believe that under this pricing scheme they will pay less for their use of air traffic control services and that business jets will pay more. The private- and corporate-jet owners prefer a fuel tax and argue that they should not pay higher fees because they cost the FAA less to handle than do the commercial airlines. Of course, general aviation planes that operate off-peak (for example, "weekend warriors" as opposed to business travelers) would pay little under congestion pricing for airspace. Instead of mediating the debate, the FAA should focus on how current pricing inefficiencies are contributing to travel delays and develop a cost-based pricing scheme. As this chapter is being completed, the FAA reauthorization bill has not been passed by Congress—funding has been provided by a series of short-term extensions—and the draft legislation that the House of Representatives and the Senate have crafted offer no improvements in the efficiency with which air traffic control is funded.

INVESTMENT. As noted, the FAA hires air traffic controllers and other air traffic control personnel and supplies terminal and en route facilities with new equipment. Personnel and equipment tend to be added to those parts of the

34. Matthew L. Wald, "FAA Seeks New Source of Revenue in User Fees," *New York Times,* March 7, 2006.

system where traffic levels exceed a threshold. The FAA's allocation of funds is also influenced by airlines, airports, trade associations, and members of Congress, a process that may compromise the efficiency of FAA investments.

Morrison and Winston (2008b) document at least one way that FAA investments could be improved. Compared with the current allocation, they find that allocating expenditures to towers and TRACONs serving airports where travelers incur the most costly delays would generate more than $1 billion in annual time savings to air travelers and cost savings to airlines. Under the current allocation, smaller airports get a disproportionately large share of funds, an allocation that appears to be zealously protected by representatives of the districts where the airports are located. For example, Oster and Strong (2006) point out that when the Air Traffic Organization proposed in February 2005 to close control towers between midnight and 5:00 a.m. at forty-eight lightly used airports, U.S. legislators from the airports' districts strongly opposed the action without considering whether the tower services were needed or even used.

Robyn (2007) finds that, despite the FAA's investments to modernize air traffic control technology, controller productivity (as measured by instrument-flight-rule operations per controller) has not improved during the past twenty-five years, and production costs have grown significantly. Productivity could have improved if many of the routine tasks that controllers perform were performed by new hardware and software. For example, it is possible and desirable to automate the handoff of a flight from one sector to another, especially because this task accounts for a large share of all air-to-ground communications.

TECHNOLOGY ADOPTION. The FAA could also reduce delays by expeditiously implementing technologies that have the capability of expanding navigable airspace around airports and en route. I have indicated that the FAA has yet to fully adopt the air traffic control technology that was envisioned when the advanced automated system was initiated during the early 1980s. Worse, the technology is no longer state of the art. By enabling pilots to be less dependent on controllers and to choose the most efficient altitude, routing, and speed for their trip, the NextGen satellite-based system could reduce air travel times and carrier operating costs, especially those related to fuel, and handle more traffic while maintaining, if not improving upon, the nation's air transportation safety record. In fact, the NextGen system would facilitate the first significant change from the air traffic routes established in the 1920s, when the government was developing airmail service. Today's pilots, while flying at much higher altitudes than they did several decades ago, still follow the same routes.

Unfortunately, the delays that the FAA has experienced with implementing experimental satellite-based systems suggest that NextGen will take more than the projected twenty-five years to become fully operational and that the current system may eventually have to impose additional delays on aircraft to handle growing traffic volumes safely. The GAO has concluded that the FAA has failed to provide the expertise to make the transition to NextGen and has urged it to seek assistance from a third party.[35] Calvin L. Scovel III (2008), the inspector general of the DOT, has identified concerns that the FAA is not properly organized to manage or execute a multibillion-dollar effort. Scovel recently told a congressional panel that the En Route Automation Modernization computer system, a critical underpinning of NextGen, has run into serious problems that will delay deployment of the new air traffic control system.[36]

Finally, all the facilities associated with the current system will eventually be eliminated or consolidated as NextGen is managed and operated with fewer and more technologically up-to-date facilities. Such disinvestment and consolidation will undoubtedly face political resistance that slows the implementation of NextGen because members of Congress will attempt to keep current navigational aids and jobs in their districts.[37]

Summary and Conclusions

Air travelers in the United States have never been safer—and they have never suffered such long delays on their flights. As summarized in table 5-2, inefficient pricing and investment policies toward airports and air traffic control have significantly contributed to delays that are costly to travelers and carriers.[38] Travelers and carriers are also harmed by federal agencies' slow adoption of technologies and practices to improve security and air traffic control, while other inefficient airport policies have reduced competition and raised fares.

Despite air transportation's strong safety record, Representative James Oberstar, chairman of the House Transportation Committee, has recently criticized the FAA for allowing a "carrier-favorable, cozy relationship" to set in—raising concerns that the agency may be compromising safety. Such

35. "FAA Urged to Seek Help with NGATS," *Flight International,* August 1, 2006.

36. Joan Lowy, "Problems Plague New Air Traffic Control Computers," *Associated Press,* April 22, 2010.

37. David Hughes, "FAA Accelerates Performance-Based Navigation, Outlines Mandates," *Aviation Week,* July 30, 2006; Dick Armey, "Fixing the Air Traffic Mess," *Wall Street Journal,* August 20, 2007.

38. Inclement weather, which policymakers cannot control, also contributes to travelers' delays. But its effect interacts with carriers' operations, airports' runway capacities, and the like.

Table 5-2. *Aviation Infrastructure Policies and Their Inefficiencies*

Policy	Inefficiency
Airport runway pricing	Weight-based landing fees undercharge aircraft for their contribution to delays during peak periods, increasing travelers' delay costs and airlines' operating costs.
Airport slot controls to limit operations	Slot controls have tended to reduce competition and raise fares.
Airport runway investment	Regulatory hurdles significantly increase the time and cost to build new runways and extend existing runways, which could reduce delays.
Airport gate utilization	Limited availability of gates reduces competition and raises fares.
Airport security	Screening procedures could be implemented at much lower cost and cause travelers much shorter delays.
Air traffic control pricing	The ticket tax does not vary with air space congestion; thus aircraft are undercharged for their contribution to delays, which increase travelers' delay costs and airlines' operating costs.
Air traffic control investments	Funds for air traffic control facilities are not allocated to minimize delay costs, which forfeits potential savings to travelers and carriers.
Air traffic control technology adoption	The FAA does not adopt new technologies in an efficient, expeditious manner, thus increasing the costs of the system and preventing users from incurring lower delay costs.

Source: Author.

concerns are greatly exaggerated, especially because the market and the liability system provide strong incentives for air carriers to behave in a socially beneficial manner. In addition, because the airlines and aircraft manufacturers know far more about aircraft technology and airline operations than the FAA does, FAA air safety regulations do not appear to be indispensable.[39] If privatization of aviation infrastructure would not compromise air safety, it would be worthwhile to explore whether it could reduce the inefficiencies of the national aviation system.

39. Dominic Gates, "FAA Lets Aerospace Firms Certify Safety of Their Products," *Seattle Times,* September 2, 2008, reports on a new regulatory program where certain manufacturers have been approved by the FAA to self-certify the safety of their products.

6

Constraints on Efficient Reforms

Policymakers experience most of the same shortcomings in the nation's transportation system that other travelers experience, so it is natural to ask why they do not make greater efforts to improve travel for all Americans.[1] One reason is that agency limitations and regulatory constraints make it extremely difficult for would-be reformers to rid any part of the system of its major inefficiencies. Of course, politicians are willing to fight for near-"Pareto" policy improvements, which benefit a vast majority of their constituents and impose small—and possibly escapable—losses on other potential voters. But political forces impede such improvements in the transportation sector because inefficient policies redistribute significant resources to many diverse and influential interest groups that may be worse off if efficient policy reforms are implemented. At the same time, many of the costs of inefficient policies are widely shared by taxpayers, who may not be aware of them or may not find them sufficiently onerous to actively support comprehensive transportation reform.

Institutional Constraints

Federal and state transportation departments and agencies play an important role in how transportation systems perform on a daily basis. Unfortunately, those government organizations are unable to make efficient policy reforms because of their inflexibility, short-sightedness, and conflicts. At the same time, they are able to deflect blame for the current state of affairs because they are entangled in a decisionmaking process with diffused accountability.

---

1. After a frustrating trip from Detroit to Washington, D.C., that took twenty-two hours and two airlines to complete, Senator Jim Bunning suggested that the airline industry should be reregulated, but he never proposed any legislation to that effect.

At the heart of the inefficiencies in airports and air traffic control is the Federal Aviation Administration (FAA), which lacks organizational independence and is prevented to a significant extent by Congress and the administration from using its resources—and from encouraging airports to use theirs—more efficiently. For example, the Transportation Security Administration's shortcomings can be traced partly to the political objective of Congress and the Department of Homeland Security to convince the public that they are doing something to combat terrorism, even if some of their efforts are wasting resources.

Constructive reforms must also overcome various regulations. Widespread adoption of runway congestion pricing would require airline tenants and their airport landlords to abrogate their existing residual and compensatory contracts and to develop an acceptable framework for determining all airport charges;[2] efficient expansion of airport runway capacity is impeded by regulatory hurdles imposed by federal environmental regulations and by opposition from local communities; and "majority in interest" clauses permit incumbent airlines to block construction of new terminals and gates that could enable new entrants to serve the airport.

Federal and state highway and transit agencies do little to assess whether the vast public expenditures on urban transportation have been spent efficiently. The Government Accountability Office (GAO 2005b) concluded that retrospective cost-benefit evaluations of highway and transit projects were not usually conducted to determine whether proposed outcomes were actually achieved, even though the outcomes were important reasons why the projects were pursued. Transportation officials told GAO that little incentive exists for them to direct available funding to performing outcome evaluations, but they also said that potential risks do exist from finding out that a project is not providing the intended benefits. Thus, because government measures inputs instead of outputs in many venues, transportation agencies tend to declare that a project is a success once it is operating.

Political Forces

Public regulations and expenditures are likely to benefit particular stakeholders, especially those who pressure members of Congress and regulatory officials to support their agenda. Political pressure by lobbyists can be observed directly and is also the source of conflicts between policymaking

2. As noted in the preceding chapter, Levine (2007) points out additional legal issues that a runway congestion pricing policy would have to address before it could be implemented.

bodies (such as the House of Representatives and the Senate), modes (for example, the automobile and public transit), and system users (such as general aviation and commercial airline carriers). Inefficient transportation policies are largely the result of policymakers' collective assessments of how best to respond to those pressures to advance their political objectives.

Opposition to Efficient Pricing Reforms

Generally, it is rare to find transportation policymakers calling for efficient pricing reforms, but former secretary of transportation Mary Peters was an exception—only to encounter strong resistance from members of Congress and state and local officials. For example, Secretary Peters supported congestion pricing as a way to fix the nation's highway infrastructure without substantially increasing federal spending and dramatically raising fuel taxes. Representative James Oberstar, chairman of the House Transportation and Infrastructure Committee, called that policy "narrow, myopic, uninspired, and fragmented," while Representative Peter DeFazio, chairman of the House Highway and Transit Subcommittee, said that funds raised from congestion pricing should be dedicated to urban transit and not to highways, so that the "factory line worker" has options.[3]

As part of a Transportation Department initiative to encourage metropolitan areas to conduct congestion pricing experiments, Secretary Peters hoped to disburse $354 million in federal funds to help implement Mayor Michael Bloomberg's plan to charge motorists $8 and trucks $21 to enter Midtown and Lower Manhattan during the busiest hours on weekdays. (Strictly speaking, the charge amounted to a cordon fee instead of congestion pricing because it did not vary with traffic volume throughout the day.) But a complex set of political factors—including but not limited to the opposition of Sheldon Silver, the influential New York Assembly Speaker—derailed the plan, and it was never approved by the state legislature.[4]

The FAA estimates that more than 50 percent of airline delays nationwide originate from the New York area airspace. Secretary Peters tried to address this problem by calling for the federal government to conduct auctions that would enable up to 10 percent of the takeoff and landing slots at the three

3. Colby Itkowitz, "The Great Highway Debate: It All Comes Down to Money," *Congressional Quarterly*, February 13, 2008. Winston and Shirley (1998) indicate that public transit has not facilitated lower-income workers' access to jobs.

4. As Schaller (2010) discusses, the public, as indicated by opinion polls, and the New York City Council supported the plan, but a relatively small group of auto users opposed congestion pricing and, given the extensive approval process, found an avenue to block action.

major New York–area airports, Kennedy, LaGuardia, and Newark-Liberty, to be claimed by the highest bidder. The auctions were expected to lessen congestion and delays at the three airports and consequently at other airports because airlines would reduce the cost of the slots per passenger by using larger planes to haul more passengers per flight, thereby using fewer regional jets and reducing the total number of flights. At the request of Jet-Blue Airlines, New York's Governor David Paterson and Senator Charles Schumer ignored the economic justification for the plan and sided with the Air Transport Association in attacking it as illegal and ideologically driven.

Stiglitz (1998) described his efforts, as part of the Clinton administration, to institute peak-period pricing for air traffic control only to find reform blocked by owners of corporate jets and small planes who opposed higher user fees. The FAA and commercial airlines appear to support replacing the ticket tax with user fees—although commercial airlines are opposed to congestion pricing. In any case, the current funding mechanism is supported by the potent National Business Aviation Association and the National Air Traffic Controllers Association; hence, it is unlikely that the next aviation reauthorization bill will significantly reform the way aircraft are charged for their use of controlled air space.

Congressional Spending on Transportation

Because federal transportation legislation reauthorizes hundreds of billions of dollars for aviation and surface transportation spending that has the potential to benefit certain stakeholders at the expense of others, members of Congress have engaged in contentious negotiations to craft the legislation. In recent years Congress has failed to meet fiscal year deadlines for passing the highway and aviation reauthorization bills because the House and Senate could not resolve their differences over spending levels and priorities. Congress has therefore had to pass continuing resolutions to prevent aviation and highway spending from grinding to a halt.

Notwithstanding members' protracted debates about the size and composition of transportation bills, Congress has reached a compromise that has resulted in using crude formulas that inefficiently apportion federal highway funds to the states and federal aviation funds to air traffic control facilities, instead of using a cost-benefit approach to allocate those funds efficiently to alleviate the country's most congested highways and air travel corridors. Inefficiencies are magnified because expenditures on specific projects reflect compromises made by state authorities to adjudicate the competing interests of local authorities.

Finally, Congress also opposes cost-effectiveness criteria for New Starts transit projects such as the Minneapolis light rail system. And members resist efforts to eliminate and consolidate air traffic control facilities to implement the NextGen system.

Interest Groups

Special interest politics is transparent in several areas of transportation policy. Dilger (2009) points out that through their public interest groups, state and local government officials have lobbied for increased federal assistance for surface transportation grants and increased flexibility in how they use those funds. Active interest groups include but are not limited to the National Governors Association, National Conference on State Legislatures, National Association of Counties, National League of Cities, U.S. Conference of Mayors, and the American Association of State Highway and Transportation Officials.

Representatives of motorists and truckers, the American Automobile Association and the American Trucking Association, oppose efficient congestion tolls and axle-weight charges that are likely to cause many of their members to pay more for using the road system. Labor unions oppose removing Davis-Bacon regulations because thousands of construction workers would see their wages fall. Highway spending responds to interest groups, as evidenced by ever greater expenditures on demonstration projects that benefit construction companies, engineers, unions, city planners, and so on. Evans (1994) has shown that the inclusion of pork barrel (demonstration) projects has become important to securing passage of the federal legislation that reauthorizes highway and transit spending. Nash (2007) concludes that politicians find road construction projects attractive because they satisfy both constituents in general as well as powerful interest groups.

The subsidies that have become a fixture in urban transit largely accrue to powerful interests—higher wages to labor, including managers, operators, and station agents; and higher profits to suppliers of transit capital. A portion, however, does go to keeping fares below cost and to expanding service beyond the level that could be supported without subsides. Winston and Shirley (1998) link much of transit's pricing and service inefficiencies to patrons' political influence: upper-middle-income rail riders benefit from more frequent service and route coverage, lower- and middle-income bus riders get more frequent service, and so on.

Lobbying groups have also been formed to support specific transit projects. For example, the Dulles Corridor Rail Association led the successful effort to persuade the Federal Transit Administration to commit federal funds to extend the Washington Metro through Tysons Corner, Virginia, to Dulles airport and beyond. The association's sponsors primarily consist of businesses that provide employment and housing along the Tysons-Dulles corridor. The Obama administration's high-speed rail initiative has launched the Midwest High-Speed Rail Coalition and the Western High-Speed Rail Alliance to lobby for projects in their regions of the country.

Transit inefficiencies might be more easily overlooked if they redistributed income from the affluent to the poor, but with the average annual household income of bus and rail commuters exceeding or close to average annual household incomes, as noted previously, and with train operators and station agents for the BART system in San Francisco and union workers for New York's MTA being paid some $65,000 a year along with generous pension and health benefits, the poor are hardly transit's greatest beneficiaries.[5] In fact, the urban mobility of low-income riders is barely a consideration under the New Starts criteria for implementing a transit project.

Lobbying groups also formed a broad coalition to support a national policy of increasing transportation spending as part of the economic stimulus package. The 2009 legislation, which allocates some $50 billion for roads, bridges, and public transit without giving attention to any of the inefficiencies discussed here, was supported by the American Road and Transportation Builders Association, Associated General Contractors of America, National Association of Manufacturers, American Public Transit Association, American Society of Civil Engineers, U.S. Conference of Mayors, and a host of local governments. As noted, the economic justification for some of the projects is already being questioned.[6]

Finally, lobbying by national associations tends to have a status quo bias to avoid conflict within the association. Thus, congestion pricing that would

5. Salaries for BART train operators and station agents are reported in Patrick Hoge, "BART Pay Ranks High for Transit Workers," *San Francisco Chronicle,* July 3, 2005; salaries for MTA workers are reported in Nicole Gelinas, "New York's Subway Woes Could Have Been Avoided," *Wall Street Journal,* April 25, 2009. Winston and Shirley (1998) note that public transit's reverse commuting program, which was designed to give lower-income people greater access to suburban jobs, did not meet with much success.

6. Lori Montgomery, "Critics Say Roads Projects Won't Jump-Start Economy," *Washington Post,* October 30, 2008, reports that in response to concerns raised by economists that highway infrastructure projects are slow to develop and take too long to stimulate the economy, Representative Oberstar said that "the trouble with those economists is that they've never had their hands on a number two shovel. They've never had a callus on their hands among them. We know that we can put people to work in projects that are ready to go, designed, engineered, right-of-way acquired, and environmentally cleared. All they need is the money."

likely benefit large trucking companies is opposed because smaller trucking operations fear that the policy would put them at a competitive disadvantage. Associations that represent states are unwilling to support reforms that would improve highway financing because they fear less populated states may be worse off.

Conclusion

Because commercial airports, air traffic control, highways, and urban transit are owned and managed by the public sector, it is not surprising that policy toward those services has been strongly influenced by political forces. Unfortunately, those forces as well as institutional constraints have caused operations of and investments in aviation and highway infrastructure and urban transit service to be very inefficient and in all likelihood to remain that way as long as the public sector is responsible for their provision. Status quo bias toward inefficient policies—and against efficient policy reforms—clearly exists; for example, members of Congress and special interests continue to oppose replacing the gasoline tax and weight-based landing fees with efficient pricing schemes such as highway congestion tolls and airport slot auctions.

Increasing public dissatisfaction with highway and airport congestion and delays indicates that transportation inefficiencies have a political cost because they will not be tolerated indefinitely, thereby providing an opportunity for policymakers to propose efficient reforms. For example, after many years of doing little about their highway congestion problems, policymakers in Los Angeles and Atlanta responded to major business groups and supported high-occupancy-toll (HOT) lanes despite opposition in Congress.[7]

Of course, efficient reforms must be politically acceptable in their own right—meaning that they must be credibly sold to the public as near-Pareto improvements (that is, almost everyone will be better off and few will be worse off).[8] Researchers have tried to craft such policies by explicitly including some form of redistribution. For example, King, Manville, and Shoup (2007) report that suggestions to "buy" public support of congestion pricing include rebating toll revenues directly to motorists, spending the revenues

---

7. Although HOT lanes result in inefficiencies because the other lanes are not priced, they nonetheless represent an important first step toward congestion pricing.

8. Schaller (2010) argues that the failure of road pricing to be implemented in New York City indicates that such programs must be formulated so that drivers see tolls or fees as making them better off.

on public transportation or roads, and their own suggestion of distributing the revenues to cities with toll highways. They conclude that congestion pricing will be implemented when it is irresistible to the prospective winners.[9] But with the exception of former transportation secretary Mary Peters, high-level public sector officials have not tried to sell congestion pricing or any other efficient transportation policy reforms as attractive to society overall and to individual users of the transportation system.

Highway inefficiencies may be ignored by the public to some extent because highways are productive assets: they offer huge value (consumers' surplus) to their users even compared with their excessive costs (Semmens 2006). Winston and Shirley (1998) estimate that the annual net benefits to single-occupant auto travelers and carpoolers—that is, the benefit to motorists compared with their best alternative mode—exceed $200 billion. A similar argument can be made for airports because the value of air travel is also considerable (Morrison and Winston 1986). Winston and Shirley find that users' value of urban bus and rail transit is small (less than $10 billion); but, as in the case of Amtrak, riders may strongly value their subsidies while their cost to taxpayers is not large enough to draw much public attention.[10]

Although the political climate for efficient reforms appears to be unfavorable, one must not forget that Congress passed intercity transportation deregulation despite formidable opposition. In the case of airline and railroad deregulation, Keeler (1984) and Peltzman (1989) argue that interest groups—that is, the carriers themselves—eventually realized that it was in their interest to support deregulation. However, trucking deregulation did not occur because the motor carriers supported it. In fact, the carriers' and unions' opposition had to be overcome—which it was by a national deregulatory movement sold by its proponents as a policy to reduce inflation (Robyn 1987).

Are there signs that interest groups might realize that certain efficient reforms are in their interest or that macroeconomic conditions may spur such reforms? I postpone my comments about interest groups' preferences until later but note here that policymakers have become concerned that they lack a reliable source of funds to maintain and improve the aging U.S.

---

9. Calfee and Winston (1998) concluded from a stated preference analysis that commuters' valuation of the travel time savings from road pricing was not affected by how the government distributed the toll revenues.

10. Consider Hartwell C. Herring's July 7, 2002, letter to the *New York Times Magazine:* "The Amtrak subsidy . . . is one of the few direct benefits I get from the federal taxes I pay . . . and I need my train service."

transportation system and that the recent recession has increased those concerns. Privatization could attract firms' investments to prevent the system from deteriorating further and to provide financial relief to a public sector that is facing staggering budget deficits for the foreseeable future. Privatization could also offer an additional source of sorely needed economic growth. Hence, in a "reversal of fortune," an economic crisis may influence policymakers to explore the merits of privatization.

Privatization and Deregulation:
Evidence of Economic Effects
and Implementation

7 | Lessons from Deregulation of Intercity Transportation

The first part of this book makes clear what government intervention in the transportation system has going against it. Those drawbacks provide a starting point for what private sector involvement in the system may have going for it. Of course, private sector involvement may have its own drawbacks, so I now turn to a balanced assessment of privatization and deregulation—a transformative policy where the government transfers (through a sale) the remaining parts of the U.S. transportation system that it owns and operates to private firms and does not explicitly regulate those firms' prices, service, and the expansion and contraction of their networks (entry and exit). The government would retain some control over firms' exit through the application of bankruptcy and merger and acquisition laws and would still regulate safety and environmental standards.

With the exception of transferring the northeast freight rail system, Conrail, back to the private sector, the United States has not had recent experience with privatizing any part of the transportation system. But its recent experience with partially deregulating intercity transportation—railroads, trucking, airlines, and buses—offers an opportunity to accurately assess the economic effects of that policy. Recent leases of highway facilities to the private sector, which are subject to regulations, are far more restrictive than the privatization policy I am exploring. By taking a long-run view of deregulation—that is, by focusing not just on where the intercity transportation system has been but where it is going—the lessons from deregulation provide a useful starting point for thinking about the potential long-run effects of privatization.

Two important considerations should guide interpretations of the evidence from deregulating the U.S. intercity transportation system. First, because regulation and deregulation of a transportation mode can never occur at the same time at the national level,[1] the most accurate way to measure the economic effects of deregulating a transportation industry is a counterfactual analysis that estimates the price, cost, and service changes that are attributable solely to deregulation and thus *would not have occurred* had the industry still been regulated. Second, as discussed previously, the intercity transportation industries are still subject to some government regulations, and some, if not all, firms that were subject to regulation have not fully shed their regulatory-bequeathed operating practices and capital structure.

It is therefore useful to distinguish between the short-run and long-run effects of deregulation on the performance of an intercity transportation industry. In the short run the industry has not been completely deregulated and may be subject to other government policies that compromise its performance under (partial) deregulation. In addition, firms that existed in the industry before deregulation have not fully adjusted their operations and investments to the deregulated environment. In the long run the industry is fully deregulated and firms have optimized their operations and investments in this environment.

The Short-Run Effects of Deregulation

Beginning with the 1978 Airline Deregulation Act, prices, service, entry, and exit in the intercity transportation industries were substantially deregulated. However, travelers are still experiencing the short-run effects of airline deregulation because carrier competition and operations have been constrained by the lack of available gates at some congested airports; inefficient airport pricing and investment have allowed travel delays to grow, especially at hub airports, which handle far more operations under deregulation than they did under regulation; various hearings on and potential regulatory interventions in airline service and competition have partly diverted management's focus from improving carrier operations; and tensions between managers of legacy carriers and labor continue to exist because the "rent sharing" mentality that developed under regulation has continued under deregulation.[2]

---

1. Regulated and unregulated transportation and other markets can and have simultaneously existed at the state level. Comparisons of prices and service across states with different regulatory policies have been used to predict and assess the effects of deregulation.

2. Airline carriers were able to earn excess profits because regulation elevated fares and prevented entry. Labor unions' wage and work-rule demands reflected their desire to share in carriers' rents. Deregulation has made it much more difficult for carriers to earn excess profits, but labor and the legacy carriers still have an adversarial relationship that can be traced to their hard-fought negotiations during regulation. Carriers that entered the airline industry after deregulation have had to contend much less with this history when they negotiate with labor.

The nation is still experiencing the short-run effects of railroad deregulation because maximum rate guidelines have not resolved the captive shipper problem; the threat of a stricter form of rate regulation has at times diverted the attention of rail managers from improving carriers' operations; and railroads have not completed the task of optimizing their networks and realizing greater economies of density by abandoning and consolidating the extensive track network that was built under regulation and by building new lines to serve high-volume shippers. And the nation is still experiencing the short-run effects of trucking deregulation because inefficient highway pricing and investment have increased delivery times and reduced their reliability, making it more difficult for truckers to provide high-quality service to facilitate shippers' just-in-time inventory policies.

Despite being adversely affected by the lingering effects of regulation and deficient infrastructure, the intercity transportation industries have significantly improved their efficiency under deregulation and benefited users.[3] The key steps in the industries' adjustment process include greater competition from new entrants and from expanded entry by incumbent firms, and the freedom and economic incentives to improve operations and service quality to users. Deregulation also has its critics who point to financial crises, losses to labor, degradations in service, and the like as indicative of its failings.

Entry and Price Changes

Intercity transportation firms compete at the market or route level. It is often thought that the number of firms in a market is the best indication of the level of competition, but deregulation showed that firms' strategies may be as important as, if not more important than, the number of firms.

The deregulated airline industry experienced an increase in competition because more (equivalent-sized) carriers competed on air routes over given distances and because the presence of new, low-cost (low-fare) carriers, such as Southwest Airlines, slowly grew over time. Morrison and Winston (2000) found that the presence of Southwest sharply reduced fares on routes that it serves, on routes that it could potentially serve (that is, Southwest serves one or both of the airports on the route but not the route), and on routes where it supplies adjacent competition (that is, Southwest serves origin and

---

3. Morrison and Winston (1999) summarize the empirical evidence on the economic effects of airline, railroad, and trucking deregulation. Borenstein and Rose (2007) and Winston (2006) provide recent surveys of the evidence for airlines and railroads, respectively. Much less empirical evidence is available for the economic effects of intercity bus transportation.

destination airports that are within, say, fifty miles of the origin and destination airports that make up a given route).

Competition increased in the deregulated LTL (less-than truckload) trucking industry because of the growth of low-cost (nonunion) regional carriers and because of increased competition from alternative small shipment carriers such as UPS and Federal Express. The TL (truckload) sector has always consisted of unregulated competitors in the form of private trucking (for example, a manufacturing firm was always able to use its own trucks and drivers to ship its products.) Still, competition in this sector intensified following deregulation because national megacarriers (also called advanced truckload carriers), such as Schneider National and Landstar, developed and because private carriers could include other firms' freight among their cargo.

With the exception of the expansion of Canadian National Railway and Canadian Pacific Railway into the northern tier of the United States, no large railroad has entered the U.S. industry since deregulation. Nonetheless, railroads have had to contend with additional competition provided by advanced truckload carriers, and they have enhanced their competitiveness by accelerating the development of intermodal (truck-rail) service. Moreover, competition among railroads has increased because a large fraction of deregulated rail traffic moves under contract rates, thereby enabling shippers in many instances to play one railroad off against another when they negotiate rates.

In the most intense case, two railroads compete directly for a shipper's traffic if their tracks traverse directly into the shipper's plant or if they have access to the shipper through reciprocal or terminal switching. As Grimm and Winston (2000) point out, shippers captive to one railroad may benefit from locational competition supplied by a nearby carrier. For example, a shipper may be served by Railroad A but could threaten to locate a new facility on or build a spur line to Railroad B as a bargaining chip to obtain a lower rate from Railroad A or to get Railroad B to commit to a reduced rate. Shippers could also stimulate railroad competition in some cases through product or geographic competition. For example, an industrial site served only by Railroad A in a given market may be able to use a substitute product shipped from a different origin by Railroad B, or the site could obtain the same product from an alternative origin served by Railroad B. Finally, small shippers that may not be able to get railroads to compete intensely for their traffic may improve their bargaining position through third-party logistics firms, which achieve cost savings for shippers by leveraging the volumes of all their clients to obtain discounts from carriers.

Consumers have benefited from lower prices generated by new sources of competition in the intercity transportation industries, including incumbent firms, new entrants, and alternative modes. And those gains have been magnified because competition has also caused firms to operate more efficiently and to pass on much of the cost savings to consumers in lower prices. Deregulated competition has been sufficiently intense to cause airline fares on low-traffic-density (nonhub) routes to fall (Morrison and Winston 1997) and to cause rail fares to approach long-run marginal cost in duopoly markets for coal transportation (Winston, Dennis, and Maheshri 2009).

Improvements in Operations and Service

Deregulation has enabled intercity transportation carriers to improve the efficiency of their operations and their service to travelers and shippers simultaneously. Freed from entry and exit regulations, airlines have accelerated the development of hub-and-spoke route networks that feed travelers from all directions into a major hub airport from which they take connecting flights to their destinations. Carriers use hub-and-spoke route systems to increase load factors and reduce average costs and, by increasing the number of feasible flight alternatives, to offer travelers much greater service frequency. For example, an additional aircraft departure from a spoke airport to a hub airport can increase the number of flight alternatives on many connecting routes.

Airlines have improved the prediction capabilities of their revenue (yield) management systems of how many passengers will show up for a flight, which has reduced travelers' as well as airline costs from overbooking. In 2009, 13 of every 10,000 passengers were bumped on domestic flights, down from over 20 per 10,000 passengers in 1999.[4] Despite this improvement, the Transportation Department is proposing to raise the minimum compensation more than 50 percent for passengers denied boarding because of overbooking. If the rule takes effect, it is likely to be another example of counterproductive government intervention in intercity transportation because in response to greater compensation, airlines may substantially cut back overbooking, which may inconvenience travelers who are unable to book a particular flight that they could have actually boarded because no-shows would have enabled them to get a seat. Average load factors could also fall, raising average costs and fares.

---

4. Jad Mouawad and Michelle Higgins, "Airlines Look to Limit Bumping," *New York Times*, April 5, 2010.

Railroads have improved the design of their networks to consolidate more traffic on a given route, and they have made greater use of double-stack rail cars and intermodal operations to reduce costs and provide faster and more reliable service to shippers.[5] Trucking firms have also improved the efficiency of their networks, reduced costs, and provided faster and more reliable service to shippers.

Carriers have also made much greater efforts, sometimes with the aid of advances in information technology, to tailor their services to travelers' and shippers' varied preferences. Yield management systems have helped airlines to increase load factors by offering travelers a wide range of fares from discount fares with various travel restrictions to much higher fares with no travel restrictions. The recently unveiled Farelogix booking platform helps carriers pull up a menu of à la carte options, such as preordered meals, preferred seats, lounge access, and the like, along with different fares for different levels of frequent flyer status. Airlines' computer reservation systems have helped to improve scheduling and flight reservations. Travelers are able to access those systems on airlines' websites to book their travel, thereby obtaining the lowest discount fares, to print their boarding passes and avoid the check-in line at the airport, and to receive real-time schedule information. Further advances in information technology are enabling self-service to be less of a chore. For example, "virtual agents" help steer customers to the right page on carriers' websites.[6] It is notable that similar innovations in public transit and intercity passenger rail that could benefit travelers have rarely occurred.

Railroads and trucking firms have negotiated thousands of price-service contracts with shippers that align their services with shippers' production and inventory policies and that make more efficient use of their own capacity. For example, shippers can sharply reduce their rates—and carriers' average costs—by including backhaul shipments in their contracts. Third-party logistics firms analyze shipper distribution patterns and logistics costs and use sophisticated software to determine the lowest-cost routes and the carriers with the lowest rates. Trucks and railroads also use computer information systems to route their cargo more efficiently and to track shipments. And railroads have started to install positive train control, which uses global positioning satellites to safely reduce the spacing between trains and to enable a train to stop before an accident occurs.

---

5. Bitzan and Keeler (2007) estimate that freight railroads have reduced annual costs by as much as $10 billion from increased traffic densities attributable to deregulation.

6. Susan Stellin, "Shortcuts Define Self-Service Travel," *New York Times*, May 5, 2010.

It could be argued that carriers' adoption of advances in information technology would have occurred regardless of deregulation. But the benefits from those advances were realized because deregulated firms had the financial incentive and operating freedom to design new networks and to use the new technologies to engage effectively with customers to determine their preferences and improve service. Under regulation they had little financial incentive or competitive pressure to do so, and regulators certainly were not able to design regulations to stimulate innovative activity.

Criticisms of Deregulation

Intercity transportation deregulation has attracted its share of critics—although generally not from academia—who allege that the benefits from the policy have not been widely shared and that the deregulated transportation industries have been subject to service meltdowns and financial crises that raise questions about their long-term viability. In fact, the benefits from deregulation have been broadly shared among consumers, while the problems that firms have experienced are either part of their long-run adjustment or are not attributable to deregulation.

Price regulation benefited certain travelers by, for example, keeping airline fares below short-run marginal cost on short-haul routes and cross-subsidizing them with fares above short-run marginal cost on long-haul routes. By the same token, price regulation benefited certain shippers by preventing railroads from covering their (declining) costs by raising rates to shippers of bulk commodities, such as coal and grain, who tend to be rail captive. Thus, if economic deregulation improved pricing efficiency, it could hardly be expected to benefit every traveler and shipper. Surprisingly, in the process of improving the efficiency of the intercity transportation system, the benefits to consumers from deregulation have been more broadly distributed than expected. And for the most part, consumers' losses can be explained by economic rather than anticompetitive forces.

About 80 percent of airline passengers (accounting for 90 percent of passenger miles) fly on routes with lower average real fares since deregulation. Roughly 90 percent of the difference in the gains to travelers under deregulation can be explained by the higher costs of serving travelers on low-density routes, where smaller planes have a higher cost per seat-mile and fly with lower load factors (Morrison and Winston 1999). As noted, deregulation reduced railroad rates, on average; some small shippers have been able to share in those benefits through third-party logistics firms; and the welfare loss to captive shippers has been small. All modes have improved their service quality in the deregulated environment except when their operations have been compromised by public infrastructure inadequacies (for example, airline travel times have increased because of inefficient runway pricing and investment). Moreover, the benefits from deregulation have been achieved without compromising any mode's safety record (Savage 1999).

Labor benefited from price and entry regulation because unions' wage demands were not particularly tempered by market forces. However, consumers' gains from deregulation do not primarily consist of transfers from labor. Peoples (1998) concludes that deregulation of railroads, trucking, and airlines caused wages to fall in those industries and resulted in an annual $10.3 billion (1991 dollars) welfare loss to labor, which amounts to roughly 20 percent of the $50 billion in gains to consumers. Of course, wages were inflated above competitive levels during regulation.

A fundamental economic challenge facing the intercity transportation industries involves matching their capacity with demand. The unpredictability of demand could be particularly problematic for an industry that must invest in capacity long before actual demand materializes. If demand is lower than expected, firms may have to cut prices significantly to fill the available capacity. If demand is higher than expected, firms with the greatest capacity are likely to gain market share. The airline industry makes capacity commitments roughly two years in advance because of the lead times needed to acquire aircraft. Railroads and trucking firms face much shorter lead times when they invest in capacity. And when rail builds new track such as a spur to a factory, it typically does not do so without the firm's commitment to ship a certain amount of freight.

Since it was deregulated in 1978, the airline industry has suffered huge financial losses because of overcapacity attributable to the early 1980s and 1990s recessions and to the September 11, 2001, terrorist attacks. It has also suffered losses from the recession that began in late 2007 and from sharp increases in fuel prices in the latter part of the decade that substantially raised the cost of carrier capacity. Of course, macroeconomic contractions, terrorist attacks, and spikes in fuel prices are not caused by deregulation. In fact, industry losses may have been greater if carriers were still regulated because they would not have had the flexibility to respond to those shocks by adjusting fares and capacity throughout their networks.

Railroads are able to contract with shippers to align their cars and equipment with shippers' demand and to reduce their vulnerability to financial problems caused by overcapacity. But railroad consolidations in the aftermath of deregulation, such as the merger of Union Pacific and Southern

Pacific and the acquisition of Conrail by Norfolk Southern and CSX, have resulted in service disruptions because the acquiring carrier did not effectively integrate the acquired carrier into its operations. Fortunately, rail operations have improved quickly after the service disruptions, and, because network capacity was restored, shippers' rates have not been elevated (Winston, Maheshri, and Dennis, forthcoming). In the future one can hope that railroads involved in consolidations will take measures to avoid such disruptions.[7]

Finally, airlines have been sharply criticized for lengthy delays and in some cases for holding their passengers "hostage" on a tarmac for several hours. But as noted, air travel delays reflect to a large extent inefficient pricing and investment policies, while extreme delays suggest that an airport is indifferent toward the quality of service that its users receive. In my view, a private commercial airport would seek to develop a reputation for safeguarding travelers, in part by instituting policies that prohibit airlines from forcing passengers to remain in their aircraft for an excessive period of time (more than a few hours) before taking off and by implementing effective procedures that enable aircraft to return to the terminal to deplane passengers in the event of a protracted delay. Public airports have little economic incentive to reduce travelers' delays and discomfort and are therefore bystanders while passengers are stuck on *their* infrastructure for hours.[8]

The Long-Run Effects of Deregulation

In the long run the benefits to consumers from intercity transportation deregulation will increase because firms will no longer be saddled by three short-run constraints: suboptimal public infrastructure, counterproductive residual regulations, and inefficient practices and investments developed during the regulatory environment. The transportation industries cannot address the first and second constraints on their own. Indeed, a central goal of this book is to explore whether privatization could significantly ameliorate the first constraint. Unfortunately, even an optimistic assessment would

7. Winston, Maheshri, and Dennis indicate that future consolidations may arise if, for instance, the two remaining major carriers in the West, Burlington Northern and Union Pacific, merge with the two major carriers in the East, CSX and Norfolk Southern, to form two transcontinental railroads.

8. According to the 2009 U.S. Transportation Department T-100 on-time performance database, roughly 5 percent of delayed flights for the 100 largest metropolitan areas were delayed more than six hours.

conclude that it would take decades to do so; in other words, the full benefits of deregulation are a long way away.

For their part, the intercity transportation industries continue to adjust to the deregulated environment and improve their operations and investments. Through its travails with exogenous economic and noneconomic shocks, the airline industry has become more resilient and efficient. It is improving its ability to match capacity with demand under a variety of difficult circumstances. As noted, during the past decade airlines have reduced overbooking and denied boarding to fewer passengers. But the industry can make further strides in optimizing its capacity in the face of changes in the business cycle. In addition, its labor relations are still contentious, and it is not well positioned to compete as effectively as possible in a deregulated global airline market. When those problems are adequately addressed, U.S. air carriers will, at long last, have shed the inefficiencies of regulation, fully adjusted their operations to the deregulated environment, demonstrated that they can be profitable throughout the business cycle, and enhanced consumer welfare even further.

The railroad industry has greatly improved its financial performance under deregulation, but it has not consistently earned a normal rate of return on its invested capital.[9] To achieve that goal, carriers are slowly modernizing their equipment and optimizing their plant size by pruning their networks of unprofitable markets and investing in potentially profitable ones. Rail has also shown that it is adjusting better to changes in the business cycle. Instead of significantly cutting spending as it did in the early 2000s recession, which caused bottlenecks and delays because carriers were unable to handle the rebound in traffic, railroads have continued to invest in tracks, tunnels, equipment, and technology during the recession that began in late 2007 and have been able to offer shippers improved service as traffic increased in 2010. Rail will therefore continue to make progress in improving its service times and reliability, reducing its costs, and benefiting shippers. The industry's structure has also not fully adjusted to deregulation. It is possible that more rail mergers will be proposed until only two (highly efficient) Class I railroads remain in the industry. This end-to-end restructuring would create two transcontinental railroads but still leave two large railroads in the East and two in the West, thereby having little effect on competition. Indeed, this may be the final equilibrium for the U.S. rail freight industry.

---

9. The railroad industry's profitability is a controversial issue. However, it does appear that the industry's returns on investment have been below its cost of capital (Grimm and Winston 2000).

The trucking industry has alleviated the serious shortage of long-distance drivers by increasing the use of intermodal operations and increasing compensation. Under deregulation for-hire truckers have significantly reduced their empty mileage, and they can make further progress by continuing to consolidate loads and attracting more traffic from private trucking.[10]

Conclusions and Implications for Privatization

By relaxing the federal government's control over airlines', railroads', and truckers' pricing, entry, and exit decisions, deregulation has tried to improve social welfare by accomplishing three goals for consumers and firms: to enable them to behave more efficiently within the technological "frontier"; to enable them to behave more efficiently as firms innovate and expand the frontier; and to enable them to respond more effectively to external shocks to reduce their costs.

Deregulation of the intercity transportation system has accomplished the first goal to a significant extent: firms have improved their basic operations and reduced prices, while heterogeneous consumers have selected price-service packages that are aligned with their various preferences. Deregulation has made some progress in accomplishing the second goal as firms have successfully implemented advances in information technology to improve their operations. And firms and consumers—in particular, airlines and air travelers—have made adjustments to reduce the cost of economic shocks that have occurred since deregulation began.

Because deregulation is a long term-process, firms and consumers have not completely adjusted to it. First, regulation constrained and strongly influenced firms' operations and technology. Economists and other observers have underestimated the time that firms required to optimize their pricing and service decisions to unregulated competition; to learn how to adjust those decisions to changes in the business cycle; and to shed inefficient operating practices, technology, and counterproductive frictions with labor and their competitors that may seek to gain a political advantage. Firms that have never been regulated occasionally make erroneous and costly business decisions; not surprisingly, deregulated firms have made their share of mistakes and have required considerable time to learn from those mistakes and to

---

10. There has been little analysis of the intercity bus industry's adjustment to deregulation. But as Schwieterman (2007) notes, the industry has started to assert itself some twenty-five years after being deregulated by expanding service in several national markets.

learn how to respond to changes in their competitive and macroeconomic environment.

Second, it has been argued that regulation stymies innovation and technological advance (for example, Gallamore 1999) and that deregulation provides greater incentives and opportunities for firms to innovate. At the same time, the timing and location of technological advance is very difficult to predict. Intercity transportation technology has improved under deregulation, but even after decades of deregulation, it is likely that further innovations that would not occur under regulation will occur in the future.

Finally, the government must adjust its actions in light of deregulation. Counterproductive residual regulations, the threat of reregulation, and inefficient infrastructure policies have undermined the performance of the deregulated intercity transportation industries. Unfortunately, as I concluded in the previous chapter, policymakers are unlikely to reform those policies for the foreseeable future—which motivates the public policy question of whether the U.S. transportation system's performance could improve under privatization and (complete) deregulation.

Privatization differs from deregulation in at least two important respects. First, it would enable private firms to provide transportation services that were formerly provided by the public sector, but, unlike deregulated firms, private firms would either be new U.S. firms or foreign firms that have little if any experience competing in those services in the United States. Second, unlike deregulated firms, private firms would inherit to a large extent the public sector's operations, investments, and technology, and to a lesser extent its labor force.

The challenge of adjusting to unregulated competition is therefore likely to be even greater and fraught with more uncertainties for transportation firms in a privatized environment than it was for deregulated transportation firms. Based on the experience from intercity transportation deregulation, private firms' adjustment process—including the elimination of public sector inefficiencies, implementation of more efficient operations and technology, and the capacity to compete effectively in a changing economic environment—will be time consuming and far from error free. At the same time, given the extent of the accumulated inefficiencies and the potential for significant technological advance, the social gains from privatization of infrastructure and urban transit may be even greater than those from deregulation of intercity transportation. I now turn to the existing theory and empirical evidence to explore whether the potential benefits from privatization justify the risks.

8

Theory and Evidence on the Economic Effects of Privatization

The United States is generally thought to be the world's leading proponent of free markets and economic deregulation, but the policy of converting state-owned assets into privately managed assets gained worldwide attention following the United Kingdom's privatization program that was initiated by the Thatcher government in the early 1980s. As Roland (2008) observes, the privatization movement was not motivated by a well-developed theoretical argument supported by persuasive empirical evidence. Roland notes that general equilibrium theory and traditional industrial organization say little about the effect of firm ownership on economic welfare.

Traditional welfare economics indicates that public provision of goods and services is justified by market failure—but an important qualification, as illustrated by my discussion of transportation, is whether government failure is a more serious problem than market failure. Indeed, my view is that the historical case for public takeover of transportation in the United States was weak and that the evidence of government failure has been overwhelming. Broad retrospective assessments of privatization in many countries (Megginson and Netter 2001) and detailed case studies for New Zealand (Barry 2004) have concluded that it generally has had positive effects on efficiency; however, the global privatization movement has not spurred the United States to privatize its public enterprises.

Given the extensive evidence of government failure in the U.S. transportation system, privatization is a potentially constructive reform. At the same time, I must acknowledge that relying extensively on the private sector to provide transportation service and infrastructure creates the risk of market failure attributable to the abuse of monopoly power or inadequate management of uncertainty in demand, costs, and the like that could lead to a financial collapse.

In this chapter, I summarize how economic theory that has been developed since the global privatization movement began sheds some light on the likely outcome of the trade-off between government failure and the risk of market failure. I then discuss the available theoretical and empirical evidence on the likely economic effects of privatizing the major components of the U.S. transportation system.

General Theory

Privatization policies throughout the world and in some theoretical discussions have included a potential role for the government to regulate the prices and service of privatized firms under some circumstances. I have argued that residual regulation in the partially deregulated intercity transportation industries has tended to be counterproductive, so I focus in this chapter on a "pure" privatization policy that has no economic role for the public sector other than to enforce antitrust, antifraud, and other general business laws and to set standards for safety and environmental regulations. Megginson and Netter (2001) and Vickers and Yarrow (1991) discuss alternative methods for selling or distributing state-owned assets to private firms, but I do not base my discussion on any particular method.

Government ownership of firms is not justified in a market that would be perfectly competitive. If the industry is a natural monopoly—a rare situation that exists when production costs are minimized if one firm supplies the good or service—the policy choice is between a government enterprise and a private monopoly regulated by the government. Privatization is an option for a publicly owned enterprise(s) or unregulated natural monopoly that would operate as a private firm(s) in an imperfectly competitive environment.

Roland (2008) characterizes contract-theoretic assessments of the difference between public and private ownership of firms as stressing the informational differences stemming from different forms of ownership. Government ownership reduces outsiders' access to information about a firm; hence public firms may have weak incentives to operate efficiently because they are poorly monitored. Vickers and Yarrow (1991) add that direct subsidies and cross-subsidies from public funds and regulations are easier to institute under public ownership. Private firms face capital market pressures that give them greater incentives than public firms have to innovate and reduce production costs, albeit at a potential cost to consumers in higher prices and lower product quality.

Figure 8-1. *Trade-off of Inefficiencies of Public Ownership and Private Monopoly*

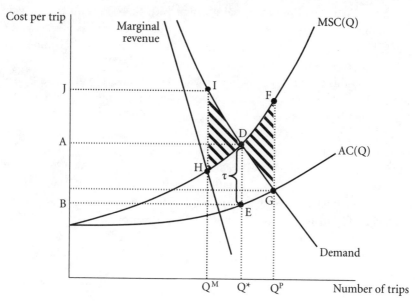

Source: Author's depiction.

Thus, whether privatization is superior to public ownership on economic grounds is likely to turn on the extent of market power that a private firm(s) possesses; the extent to which incentives influence whether a firm(s) achieves its goals; and whether consumers have any recourse for applying competitive pressure on the private firm(s).

As an example of an ambiguous outcome, figure 8-1 shows the case of a highway where the average cost (*AC*) of drivers' trips is less than the marginal social cost (*MSC*) of their trips because drivers do not account for their contribution to congestion and delays when they make their travel decisions. Under optimal congestion pricing, drivers are charged a toll, τ, so that the number of trips, Q^*, is determined at the point where demand equals the *MSC* of a trip. However, as noted, public authorities do not allocate scarce highway capacity efficiently because drivers are not charged for contributing to congestion; hence road users only consider their average costs and make Q^P trips that result in a welfare loss—the difference between social costs and social benefits evaluated at the actual and optimal level of trips—given by the shaded area *DFG*. Privatization of the road is an alternative to public ownership. A profit-maximizing monopoly road provider sets a price for using the highway by equating marginal revenue with the *MSC* of a trip, which results in the number of trips given by Q^M and a welfare loss given by the shaded area *DHI* if the monopolist does not engage in price discrimination or change its prices over time.

Thus, in this example, it is not clear whether privatization that results in a monopoly highway provider raises or lowers welfare compared with a publicly owned highway that does not charge users for their congestion costs. Privatization could improve welfare if travelers could use an alternative route or mode, such as rail transit, which would put competitive pressure on the private operator to significantly reduce its monopoly price. As noted in my discussion of rail freight transportation, shippers found several ways—some of which may have been unanticipated during regulation but materialized following deregulation—to subject a monopoly railroad to competitive discipline. Privatization could also improve welfare if the private monopolist's spending of its highway revenues was more efficient than the public sector's spending of its revenues.

Another difficult trade-off to resolve a priori may occur if the privatized firm requests a subsidy because it experiences a significant financial loss caused by, for example, a long-term decline in demand. The cost of the subsidy would have to be compared with the welfare gains from privatization; alternatively, the privatized firm could enter bankruptcy.

Dynamic considerations are particularly important for assessing privatization. A potentially relevant case arises when a monopolist supplies a durable good, implying that its behavior for more than one period is of interest. Coase (1972) argues that although the monopoly price restricts output in the initial period, the monopolist has an incentive to sell the restricted (durable) output in later periods. This case contrasts with the standard static case when the monopoly price irrevocably results in a deadweight loss because output that could be sold at a price below the monopoly price is not sold. Consumers know the monopolist's incentives and will not commit to buying the high-priced output that is initially put on the market. The monopolist must therefore offer a slightly lower price than the monopoly price to sell successive units of output. Over time the (bargaining) process eventually converges when all output is sold at the competitive price. Essentially, consumer demand becomes perfectly elastic, as in a perfectly competitive industry, because the monopolist is forced to compete against itself in future periods.

The Coasian Conjecture, as it is called, has spawned a large theoretical literature that has identified favorable and unfavorable conditions for the monopoly producer to set a competitive price. Two important conditions that favor a competitive price are that the good is highly durable and faces growing demand, which makes it costly for the monopolist to hold back output or capacity.

Why is the analysis of durable goods pricing potentially relevant for transportation even though such service is perishable because it is time specific (for example, a seat on an airplane flight that departs at 9 a.m. is no longer available after the flight takes off)? Consider travelers and shippers who use a unit of transportation capacity on a regular basis—for example, every weekday a commuter drives on a highway lane at 8 a.m. to get to work, or every week a shipper fills a rail car with its cargo for a delivery to a receiver in another state. From this perspective, travelers and shippers could purchase a unit of durable transportation capacity to use repeatedly over a long period of time. In fact, the contractual equilibrium that has emerged following rail freight deregulation reflects this behavior as shippers and carriers have negotiated long-term contracts, enabling shippers to secure a unit of capacity (such as rail cars or unit trains) that is available to ship their freight on a regular basis and enabling carriers to sell as much of their capacity as possible (Meyer and Tye 1988).

The upshot of the durable goods perspective is that prices and service in a privatized transportation system could be determined through intense contract negotiations between users—possibly represented en masse by a third party—and suppliers; such contracts could enable privatization to increase social welfare even in markets where it results in a monopoly provider.[1] Contracts could also be designed to help stabilize the financial condition of a private firm should it experience an economic shock that reduces demand or increases costs.

As indicated by the evolution of U.S. industries, dynamics are also important because competition that develops over time can erode a firm's monopoly or near-monopoly position. Recent examples of dominant firms that have lost considerable market share in the past few decades include Kodak, General Motors, and U.S. Steel. The intercity transportation deregulation experience also shows how competition between new and existing firms can evolve and generate greater benefits to consumers over time.

---

1. Gomez-Ibanez (2003) characterizes a range of solutions—from private markets to public enterprise—as addressing a contracting problem with a monopolist.

Of course, regulated intercity firms competed to some extent and were better prepared for unregulated competition than are public airports, highways, and urban bus and rail systems. Indeed, chapter 7 indicated that based on the intercity transportation deregulation experience, privatization must be viewed as a long-term process. But will this process eventually result in a workably competitive transportation system that benefits consumers? I turn to the available theoretical and empirical evidence for initial guidance.

Theory and Evidence in Transportation

U.S. transportation infrastructure and urban transit have been shielded from unrestrained competitive forces for such a long time that it is natural to doubt whether a workably competitive environment could ever develop for airports, air traffic control, highways, and urban bus and rail that would raise economic welfare. However, the limited theoretical and empirical research that exists frequently—but not always—puts privatization in a favorable light and suggests that it is possible for effective competition in all the major components of the nation's transportation system to develop.

The public-private partnerships that are being formed to expand investment in airports and highways are not a particularly useful source of evidence because they are simply business deals intended to yield an acceptable rate of return for the firms that invest in infrastructure. Potential benefits to the public include budgetary relief, reduced project risks, and faster completion of projects through incentive contracting. Public-private partnerships have not typically been motivated by an interest among policymakers to develop competition in transportation services that would enhance social welfare.[2]

Highways

Recent private sector involvement in the provision of highways—although quite limited—is seen by some observers as a potential starting point for privatization.[3] Indeed, economists have long argued that roads are amenable

---

2. Public-private partnerships are also not an accurate preview of privatization's economic effects because the contract between the private firm and the government may be poorly structured (Engel, Fischer, and Galetovic 2007).

3. Private sector involvement in U.S. highways includes the Chicago Skyway, Indiana Toll Road, and the proposed Florida and Texas Trans-Corridor public-private partnerships; high-occupancy-toll lanes in California, Texas, and the Washington, D.C., metropolitan area; and the Dulles-Greenway private toll road.

to competition in a variety of situations and that they should be privatized.[4] Knight (1924) reasoned that a private road would set an optimal congestion toll if it faced competition from an alternative free (public) road. Friedman and Boorstin (1951), early advocates of privatization, suggested that the government should account for unfair competition by rebating fuel tax revenues generated by motorists driving on the free road to the private road owner. Even if the rebate does not occur, Viton (1995) found that a private road in a well-traveled urban corridor would be financially viable when competing against a public road for most types of road users. Edelson (1971) qualified Knight's result by showing that it holds if all travelers—including those using a transit alternative to the private road—have the same value of time. If travelers differ in their value of time, the toll could result in too much or too little congestion. De Palma and Lindsey (2000, 2002) and Calcott and Yao (2005) conclude that private operators have incentives to introduce time-varying tolls in alternative competitive settings.

In sum, theoretical work indicates that private highway competition could result in a wide range of outcomes. Winston and Yan (2010), by analyzing empirically motorists' highway travel on State Route 91 in California, identified more precisely certain conditions that would lead to positive welfare effects from highway privatization. The road currently consists of high-occupancy toll lanes and regular lanes, which Winston and Yan assume take the form of two routes with equal lane capacities. Competitive options include a monopolist operating the routes, duopoly competition, or a private operator competing with a public (government) operator. The essential behavioral components of the model are that the government sets a sales price for the road to maximize social welfare; road users have varying values of time and reliability and varying preferences for highway service and make utility-maximizing decisions of whether to travel on the highway and the route to use if they do travel; and private highway operators set prices (tolls) and, in the case of monopoly, allocate lane capacity to different types of road users based on their values of time to maximize profits.[5]

The authors found that highway privatization could benefit road users and increase welfare by reducing the inefficiencies associated with current (public sector) road pricing and capacity allocation, even if the highway is

---

4. Privatization appears to be feasible in part because the provision of road services is characterized by constant returns to scale (Small 1999).

5. Duopolists are assumed to have equal road capacities and are limited in their ability to allocate lane capacity to different types of road users.

owned and operated by a monopolist. I noted earlier that a contract equilibrium—where a third party represents travelers or shippers—could play an important role in privatization, and, in fact, it turns out to play a critical role in Winston and Yan's findings because a third-party representing motorists negotiates tolls and the allocation of capacity with a private highway provider(s), which responds to motorists' preferences in ways that public highway authorities do not by offering motorists a choice of paying a high toll to use lanes with little congestion or paying no toll to use lanes that are highly congested. The bargaining framework prevents a highway operator from earning monopoly profits, although an operator is able to be profitable; thus privatization potentially benefits motorists and firms. This finding does not appear to be an extreme result; the authors report a wide range of negotiated outcomes that enable both the private operator and motorists to gain from privatization. Of course, an important qualification to this finding is that privatization in practice may not lead to bargaining between a highway operator and a third party or, even if it does, the bargaining may not yield significant gains to motorists.

Privatization will also free private operators from onerous regulations and provide them with strong incentives to reduce highway production costs, especially those attributable to the damage that heavy trucks inflict on pavements. Roth (2005) reports that state highway officials estimate federal regulations raise highway project costs 20–30 percent. Poole and Samuel (2008) find that the share of toll revenues consumed by operating and maintenance costs is 43 percent for U.S. public toll roads and 23 percent for U.S. private toll roads.[6] Privatization is also likely to spur innovations in highway services.

Highway privatization has been active outside of the United States, initially in other developed countries but also in developing countries in Southeast Asia (Gomez-Ibanez and Meyer 1993). Australia's Macquarie Bank Ltd. and Spain's Cintra Concesiones have amassed large infrastructure funds and have been leading investors in private highways throughout the world. Albalate, Bel, and Fageda (2007) argue that regulations designed by public authorities in Europe have a strong influence on the welfare effects of privatization, but they do not reach a general conclusion about whether those effects are positive or negative. Roden (2006) points out that private road contractors in the

6. As communicated to me by Peter Samuel, there are examples of reasonably low-cost public toll roads with a high cost-revenue ratio because tolls have been too low (the West Virginia Turnpike has not increased its tolls since 1989, for example), but there are also examples of private operators whose tolls have been kept down by government caps (one example is the Indiana Toll Road).

United Kingdom were paid the lowest rate per vehicle-mile that they would accept to design, finance, build, and operate roads, but again he does not reach a general conclusion about privatization's welfare effects.

Urban Transit

The justification for privatizing urban transit may be questioned because as recently as the 1960s transit was primarily provided by private companies. However, the benefit of combining deregulation with privatization is that it is likely to prevent the widespread failures that occurred in the previous episode of private transit operations. Pashigian (1976) and Hilton (1985) provide evidence that private bus operations failed because they were weakened by government regulation, and Meyer and Gomez-Ibanez (1981) point out that federal policy made it almost mandatory for cities to acquire their private transit companies instead of allowing them to raise fares to remain profitable.

In response to those who claim that urban bus and rail service both exhibit economies of traffic density that could lead to destructive competition in a deregulated private market, Walters (1982) argues that the extent of those economies indicates that public transit's inefficient operating environment creates excess capacity. Such capacity, Walters says, could be substantially eliminated in a private market because operators would have the incentive and ability to improve their operations by, for example, adjusting vehicle sizes to demand. At the same time, intermodal competition—especially from the automobile—would limit the ability of bus and rail companies to exercise market power.

Winston and Shirley (1998) simulate the economic effects of privatizing and deregulating transit by constructing a model in which bus and rail companies in a metropolitan area compete with one another, as well as with private automobiles, and set prices and service frequency to maximize profits. They find that the effects of this competitive environment are very similar to the effects of marginal-cost transit pricing and optimal service frequency. The public's gains from eliminating transit deficits would substantially exceed travelers' losses from higher fares and reduced service, and private bus and rail operators would be profitable. Those findings, however, greatly overstate the potential losses to travelers because they do not reflect the improvements in operations, marketing, and service that could be achieved by private transit and the impact that new entrants would have on fares and service.

The recent limited experience with private sector involvement in transit operations in the United States and the more extensive experience with private transit operations abroad indicate the potential for privatization to generate efficiency improvements. Karlaftis and McCarthy (1999) found that Indianapolis, one of the few U.S. cities that have privatized their transit system, expanded its operations while reducing its annual operating costs roughly 3 percent. The savings from privatization are primarily efficiency gains, not transfers from transit labor. The Atlanta metropolitan area has a private bus service, known formally as Royal Bus Lines, which operates on some of the routes served by MARTA, the public provider. Anecdotal evidence indicates that the private operator's riders, the majority of whom are Hispanic, benefit from the more convenient service offered by the private option.[7]

Karlaftis (2006) and Savas and McMahon (2002) find that public transit agencies have reduced their operating costs by competitively contracting part of their services to private operators. O'Toole (2009) reports that Denver contracts out about half of its bus routes and pays contractors only 53 percent as much per bus-mile as it spends on the routes it operates. And the U.S Department of Transportation (2007) reports that public-private partnerships have reduced capital costs for rail transit projects. Finally, New Orleans plans to outsource nearly every aspect of its bus and streetcar lines to a French company, Veolia Environnement, with the hope of reducing its transit costs 30 percent; officials in Savannah are negotiating a similar contract with Veolia.[8]

Karlaftis (2006) surveys the empirical evidence on the effects of privatizing transit systems in various cities in the United Kingdom, continental Europe, Australia, Latin America, and Asia and concludes that privatization has reduced costs and increased operating efficiency, primarily through more efficient use of labor. Privatization has also spurred the use of minibuses outside London, which operate at higher speeds and offer more frequencies than conventional buses do and, because of their maneuverability, are able to stop at any point on the route to pick up and discharge passengers.

Winston and Maheshri (2007) point out that recently privatized rail transit systems in foreign cities, notably Tokyo and Hong Kong, have been able

---

7. Rachel Tobin Ramos, "Private Bus Service on a Roll," *Atlanta Business Chronicle,* January 14, 2005. As described by Miguel Helft, "Google, Master of Online Traffic, Helps Its Workers Beat the Rush," *New York Times,* March 10, 2007, Google effectively runs a small (private) transit agency by transporting part of its workforce to and from its headquarters in Mountain View, California, by bus. The system is responsive to employees' residential locations, offers state-of-the-art communications, and could be a useful model for other small private transit systems. Microsoft has also developed a bus transit system for its employees in the Seattle area.

8. Christopher Conkey, "Strapped Cities Outsource Transit Lines," *Wall Street Journal,* July 13, 2009.

to eliminate deficits by reducing labor and capital costs and by introducing more comfortable cars and remote payment mechanisms, among other innovations, that have reduced operating costs and expanded ridership.[9] Tokyo Metro's financial performance has also improved because it has generated income from nonrail business such as hotels. Recall, evidence indicates that the benefits from "transit-oriented development" in the United States are small. This finding may reflect the shortcomings of public transit authorities and indicate another way that private transit companies could enhance social welfare—either by expanding into profitable nontransit businesses or fostering commercial development close to their stations.[10]

Airports

The central tenet of airport privatization is that travelers will experience fewer delays and airline competition will increase if airports are forced to compete with each other to attract passengers and airline service. As shown in Morrison (1983), U.S. airports are not natural monopolies; in fact, airports already compete to some extent with other, nearby airports in many metropolitan areas in the United States and would compete much more intensely if they were privatized. In addition, it is likely that airlines would constrain private airports in outlying areas from exercising monopoly power by forcing them to compete to attract service.

Competition exists when multiple airports serve a metropolitan area because catchment areas are likely to overlap (Starkie 2008b) and because travelers choose among airports based on the carriers that serve an airport and the service quality that the carriers offer (Ishii, Jun, and Van Dender 2008). Some examples of markets in the United States where airports can and do compete for air travelers include Boston, Manchester (New Hampshire), Providence, and Hartford in New England; Kennedy, LaGuardia, and Newark in the New York metropolitan area; Washington, D.C. (Reagan), Baltimore (BWI), and northern Virginia (Dulles) in the Washington, D.C., metropolitan area; O'Hare, Midway, and Milwaukee (Wisconsin) in the Chicago metropolitan area; Oakland, San Francisco, and San Jose in northern

9. Stockholm currently has the only large, privately operated urban rail system in Europe. The private operator, Veolia Transport, leases the trains and the stations, while the transport authority owns the track. Robert Anderson, "Performance Targets Raise the Bar for Quality," *Financial Times*, May 18, 2007, reports that privatization has improved the quality of Stockholm's Metro rail service without increasing costs.

10. The Washington Metro recently expressed interest in putting kiosks in its rail stations that would sell retail items, but board members are stalling plans to do so.

California; and Los Angeles, Orange County, and Long Beach in southern California.[11]

The potential for competition also has been demonstrated in recent years by airports, including Boston, Dallas/Fort Worth, Fort Lauderdale, Miami, and San Francisco, which have cut landing fees and rents and contributed money for advertising to induce carriers to offer service to attractive international destinations.[12] Airports in various metropolitan areas have also competed for international flights. For example, Los Angeles airport is spending $1.2 billion to build ten new gates at an extension of its international terminal to remain competitive with San Francisco for overseas traffic.[13] Many Canadians have found it is cheaper to cross the border and use U.S. airports instead of using a Canadian airport to fly into the United States.[14] And air carriers have also induced airport competition by using other airports as leverage during contract negotiations. For example, Delta Airlines threatened to move its operations at Atlanta Hartsfield-Jackson to another airport, perhaps Memphis, unless the costs of a new international terminal and its airport fees were cut.[15] The two parties finally reached an agreement that kept Delta operating at Hartsfield.

Airport competition in certain metropolitan areas, such as New York, shows signs of increasing as satellite or local airports including Long Island's MacArthur airport, Atlantic City airport, and Stewart airport expand their operations.[16] Competition would also increase if the prohibition that keeps private airports from offering scheduled commercial service were lifted. The Federal Aviation Administration (FAA) characterizes a program that has paid hundreds of millions of dollars to owners of small airports used by private planes as easing congestion at nearby commercial hubs by handling corporate jets and recreational planes.[17] Allowing those airports to

11. Harriet Baskas, "Gloves Are Off as Airports Go after Their Rivals in Ads," *USA Today*, March 16, 2010, reports, for example, that San Francisco Airport put out a YouTube video that compared itself favorably to an unnamed "bad airport" and that Milwaukee Airport initiated an "Avoid the Chicago ORDeal" campaign, which played on the ORD airport code for Chicago O'Hare.

12. Roger Yu, "Airports Set Lures for Non-Stop Flights," *USA Today*, February 25, 2008.

13. Steve Hymon, "Council OKs 10 New Gates at LAX," *Los Angeles Times*, August 16, 2007.

14. Charisse Jones, "Some Canadians Cross Border to Fly in U.S.," *USA Today*, March 2, 2010.

15. Jim Tharpe, "Stakes High for Delta, Atlanta," *Atlanta Journal Constitution*, January 19, 2009.

16. Joseph Berger, "An Invitation to Fly Local," *New York Times*, January 3, 2010.

17. Thomas Frank, "Small Airports: Giving Us Help Benefits Everyone," *USA Today*, December 31, 2009.

serve commercial carriers would ease congestion further and, although U.S. private airports tend to be small, some would improve their facilities and could compete successfully for some commuter carrier traffic that is currently handled at major airports.

Of course, many cities are served by only one airport. Under privatization, those airports would appear to have monopoly power, which would allow them to charge excessive runway landing and takeoff prices and give them little incentive to provide high-quality services. But the ability of an airport—even if it is the only airport serving an outlying area—to exercise monopoly power is constrained by the need to be efficiently integrated into an air carrier's entire network. Thus, if an airport sets monopoly charges, a major airline may not find it optimal to include the airport in its spoke routes.[18] Or in the process of determining the routes that it will serve, an airline may be able to play off monopoly (spoke) airports against each other to reduce charges.[19] Still another option in some areas may be to establish a new airport. For example, Sioux Falls, South Dakota, is surrounded by farmland for hundreds of miles. A new airport could also be established where a military installation has closed. For example, in Southern California, San Bernardino International Airport is currently undergoing a major renovation so it can provide passenger service at the former Norton Air Force Base.[20]

It could be argued that even if an airline can limit a monopoly airport's rents from takeoff and landing fees, travelers will still pay higher fares on routes that have a monopoly airport at one or both endpoints. But the evidence indicates that the (higher) fares on low-density or nonhub routes tend to be explained by higher costs attributable to the absence of economies of aircraft size and not by an airline's monopoly power.

18. As reported by Sandra Arnoult, "CO's Kellner: Struggling Airlines Look to Serve Airports with Low Fares," *ATW Daily News*, October 14, 2009, Larry Kellner, Continental Airlines chairman, told airport executives that airports wanting to attract and retain carriers need to be cognizant of the airlines' bottom line—"the lower your cost per passenger, the likelier we will go there." Portland, Oregon, was in danger of losing all of its international nonstop routes and, as reported by Joel Millman and Mike Esterl, "Air Hubs Pay to Keep Their Spokes," *Wall Street Journal*, July 10, 2009, actually made a one-time payment of $3.5 million to Delta Air Lines to keep its nonstop route to Tokyo

19. As shown in Grimm and Winston (2000), an analogous situation occurs in rail freight transportation when an industrial firm is served by one railroad but can draw on alternative origins served by alternative railroads to receive a product. Such geographic competition has enabled shipping firms to negotiate reductions in rail rates.

20. Andrew Edwards and Joe Nelson, "Airport Execs Still Look to Land Airline," *San Bernardino County Sun*, April 10, 2010.

Intermodal competition and demand complementarities are also likely to constrain a monopoly airport's market power. Airports that serve outlying areas tend to offer air service for short-haul trips on spoke routes to major hub airports or on routes connected to smaller airports. Airport charges for such flights are limited by competition from bus, rail, and the automobile (Morrison and Winston 1985). Airports generate revenue from runway charges and parking fees and by leasing space to other businesses such as retail shops. Retailing has become a more important component of airport revenues in recent years, accounting for as much as 40 percent of overall revenue in some cities.[21] Starkie (2001) and Zhang and Zhang (2003) show that the rents from concessions improve welfare by inducing a monopoly airport to set runway charges much closer to social marginal costs—to increase passenger throughput—than if the airport had no concessions.

It may be the case that overall welfare would improve even more if the airport field and terminals were owned and operated by separate private firms because competition between terminals would cause concession rents to fall while the airport field would be subjected to the competitive forces just discussed. On the other hand, such an arrangement would eliminate any reduction in airport charges attributable to increasing the attractiveness of retail space for lease.

Finally, privatized airports would have an incentive to attract air carriers to satisfy air travelers' preferences. In particular, passengers prefer to use airports that are served by low-cost carriers and (hub) carriers that offer frequent service, so they have options in case their flight is canceled or significantly delayed. If an airport attempted to set excessive runway charges, hub and low-cost carriers might dismantle their operations and develop new ones at an alternative airport in the same or a different metropolitan area.[22] Airports would also have an incentive to work with highway and transit firms to improve their convenience for passengers and airlines. For example, Southwest Airlines was lured to Boston Logan airport, in part, because the Big Dig has significantly reduced the delays motorists encounter when they drive to Logan. One hopes that travelers in other cities would benefit from similar synergies between private airports and urban transportation

---

21. Robert Sharoff, "Indianapolis Pinning Lots of Hopes on Airport Project," *New York Times*, March 19, 2008.

22. Southwest Airlines was dissatisfied with Seattle-Tacoma airport and wanted to abandon service, but it was barred from offering service at Boeing Field. If airports were private, they would make greater efforts to attract and retain Southwest. Cleveland Hopkins provided financial incentives and additional space to persuade Continental to build a mini hub, which has resulted in more flights at the airport.

providers without incurring the exorbitant costs of the Big Dig. For example, a transit provider could expand its catchment area and patronage if it offered convenient and reliable airport service.

Although the potential exists for private airport competition to curtail the inefficient operations that have developed under public airports, direct empirical evidence is unavailable because no private commercial airports have operated in the United States for a sufficient length of time to provide an accurate assessment.[23] But evidence from simulations and from foreign countries that have partially privatized their airports offers some empirical support that privatization could benefit travelers and raise social welfare.

Morrison, Winston, and Yan (forthcoming) compare social welfare under current airport operations in the San Francisco Bay Area with privatization of Oakland, San Francisco, and San Jose airports. Although those airports are owned and operated by three separate government entities, the authors have identified possible scenarios whereby private sector competition among them and bargaining with airport users could improve traveler welfare in a contract equilibrium.

In contrast to U.S. cities, many cities throughout the world, such as London, New Delhi, Rome, Sydney, and Tokyo, have privatized their airports subject to varying degrees of regulation. In a worldwide comparison of airports, Oum, Yan, and Yu (2008) found that airport privatization has reduced costs by promoting competition. The existence of multiple airports in a metropolitan area does not improve efficiency if, as is generally the case in the United States, the airports are owned and operated by a single public authority.[24] Bilotkach and others (2010) study sixty-one European airports over an eighteen-year period and find that privatization has reduced aeronautical charges to airlines. Advani (1999) provides empirical evidence that privatized airports are much more responsive to passengers' preferences for connecting facilities, ground transport, comfortable waiting areas, and the like than are government-owned airports. To take a recent example, capsule

23. Chicago Midway Airport was the first large hub airport to apply to the FAA's airport privatization pilot program. Unfortunately, the Midway privatization experiment collapsed because the financial crisis prevented the winning bidder from raising sufficient financing to acquire the airport. But Chicago is seeking an extension to submit a proposal to privatize Midway. The cities of Austin, Detroit, Jacksonville, Kansas City, Long Beach, Minneapolis, and New Orleans, and the government of Puerto Rico, among other locations, are exploring the possibility of a private entity leasing and managing their airport. The only privately developed and operated commercial airport in the nation has recently opened in Branson, Missouri.

24. The New York region might have dealt more effectively with airport congestion if a single authority did not control all three major airports. In addition, airlines might have been better able to see the connection between airport competition and more efficient aircraft utilization.

(or pod) hotels—which enable fliers to nap between flights—are available in private airports abroad, but none is available in the United States. San Francisco airport is currently considering a concessionaire to build and operate some pod hotels in its terminals.

Case studies find that privatization has improved airport efficiency in Australia (Forsyth 2008) and the United Kingdom (Graham 2008; Starkie 2008a).[25] The leverage that airlines can place on airports was demonstrated following airport privatization in the United Kingdom. Ryanair, a European low-cost carrier, demanded that a number of U.K. airports reduce the fees they charged the carrier to zero or it would leave. Most complied, but Manchester airport did not, so Ryanair made good on its threat. Finally, competition between the two international airports in Moscow, privately owned Domodedovo and state-owned Sheremetyevo, has led to lower charges, better service, and improved facilities.[26]

Air Traffic Control

During the 1990s the Clinton administration recognized that the nation's air traffic control system was inadequate to meet the growth in airline traffic and sought to "corporatize" it by spinning off air traffic control operations as an independent government corporation that would be financed by user fees and be able to borrow money from capital markets. Congress did not support the effort, but the case for "corporatization"—and a more sweeping reform, privatization—is becoming stronger.

As Robyn (2007) points out, air traffic control is a high-technology service business that should not be trapped in a command-and-control federal bureaucracy. In fact, it should be moved outside of the traditional government bureaucracy altogether.

The shift in the air traffic control system's technology from ground-based radar to satellites and cockpit controls presents an opportunity in the future to allow competition in air traffic control service, which would improve efficiency and encourage providers to be more responsive to airspace users'

25. Privatized airports in those countries are subject to some regulations that appear to be counterproductive. In addition, the airports in London and Scotland operate under common ownership. Recently, the U.K. Competition Commission has allowed the owner of the three London airports, Ferrovial SA, to retain Heathrow Airport but required it to sell Gatwick airport. It may also have to sell Stansted airport and either Edinburgh or Glasgow airports, but that requirement is currently being resolved in court. Separate ownership of the London and Scotland airports is expected to result in beneficial competition.

26. Daniel Michaels, "Moscow Points the Way with Airport Competition," *Wall Street Journal*, December 1, 2008.

preferences.[27] Properly equipped aircraft can maintain safe distances from other planes over both land and water for most of the route without using controllers, but some supervision would still be necessary to coordinate takeoffs and landings in terminal areas. As in the case of telecommunications, competition could arise because different regional air traffic control service providers could serve different terminal areas—and enter areas that were not receiving state-of-the-art service. Providers could negotiate directly with airspace users and airports to determine the price and the type of service and equipment to be provided. As proposed by then Senator Ted Stevens, it may also be desirable to privatize procurement of facilities and equipment to facilitate their integration with operations.

Outside of the United States, many countries have restructured their air traffic control providers by granting them managerial and financial autonomy. More autonomy has caused providers to be more responsive to the preferences of the aviation community instead of treating the government as their primary client (McDougall and Roberts 2008). In a comparison of the U.S. Air Traffic Organization (ATO) with Nav Canada, a private sector air traffic control corporation established in 1996 and financed by publicly traded debt, Oster and Strong (2006) concluded that the ATO was disadvantaged by a disconnect between its source of funds and costs, the poor performance of its capital investment programs, and a lack of organizational independence that would enable it to take steps to improve its performance. The authors concluded that Nav Canada was able to overcome those problems while maintaining a high level of air safety in Canada by having the main stakeholders and users determine user fees subject to legal requirements that limit charges to full cost recovery, by undertaking modest projects that could be efficiently managed, and by having complete freedom to allocate resources and consolidate facilities when necessary.

McDougall and Roberts (2008) compared commercialized provision of air traffic control (including but not limited to Nav Canada) with the ATO's provision and found that under commercialization, safety was enhanced or unaffected, modernization of technology was greatly improved, and users benefited from improved service quality. At the same time, costs were reduced and financial stability was maintained.[28] The authors also pointed

27. The material in this paragraph is adapted from Robyn's paper.

28. Commercialization may not lead to cost minimization if providers are operating with a regulatory constraint that limits charges, earnings, or both. Nonetheless, compared with the ATO, commercialization reduced costs.

out that the ongoing procurement difficulties at the FAA, resulting in large cost overruns and delays, were typical of problems encountered by other air traffic control systems *before* they were commercialized.

Additional International Evidence on the Effects of Privatization

During the past few decades countries throughout the world have to varying degrees transferred responsibility for managing and operating their airlines and railroads from the public to the private sector. The economic effects of that change in policy provide additional perspective on the potential effects of privatization in the United States.

Two different approaches to privatization were taken in the case of railways.[29] Countries in Latin America and Japan introduced privatized railway concessions that were subject to regulations, while in Europe and Australia rail operations were unbundled from the rail infrastructure—track and stations—with different owners responsible for providing each service. Both approaches contrast with the vertically integrated and (largely) deregulated U.S. freight railroad system. The effects of the reforms have been mixed. Privatized railway concessions were generally successful in improving service for shippers and passengers and in reducing the level of public subsidy. But unbundling turned out to complicate the coordination of train operations and infrastructure maintenance, which in the case of the United Kingdom led to cost overruns, accidents, and the bankruptcy of the infrastructure company Railtrack in 2001. At the same time, although rail carriers found entry to be harder than expected, vertical unbundling did not cause serious problems in the rest of Europe and Australia. In addition, some have argued that the U.K. government deserves considerable blame for the collapse of Railtrack because it implemented the unbundling policy hastily and carelessly.

Airline market reforms throughout the world have been successful. The transformation of European aviation from a series of bilateral agreements between governments and their national airlines to a single European market has led to significant reductions in fares and improvements in productivity (Barrett 2009). As in the United States, low-cost airlines, notably Ryanair and easyJet, have contributed to the benefits of greater reliance on market forces to allocate resources in air transportation. Privatization and liberalization of airline operations has spread to Asia, Australia, and Latin America and, although the change in policy has not prevented airlines in those regions from

29. The material in this paragraph is based on the summary given by Gomez-Ibanez (2006).

experiencing financial crises primarily caused by shocks to the global economy, it has generally enabled a country's airline(s) to become more efficient.

Conclusions

Scholarly research and anecdotal evidence based on U.S. and foreign experiences indicate that privatization of highways, urban transit, airports, and air traffic control can and, in some cases, has resulted in cost savings and improved service that is responsive to users' preferences. Depending on the service and the level of public subsidies, prices may increase or decrease.[30]

While those broad findings are plausible outcomes for privatization of the U.S. transportation system, it is also important to acknowledge that positive and negative surprises from privatization can and do occur. For example, the collapse of Railtrack in the United Kingdom shows that careful implementation of privatization is crucial for its success. Unfortunately, beyond that caution, current research and experience do not provide much guidance for identifying negative surprises. At the same time, extrapolating from the deregulation experience, I would expect privatization to stimulate innovations and new technologies that improve operations, service quality, and safety; to encourage transportation users to be more engaged in indicating their preferences for various services and resourceful in avoiding excessive charges; and to attract a cadre of managers and workers who have the potential to improve the nation's transportation system substantially.

Privatization also raises concerns that have yet to be resolved in the scholarly literature and in practice. For example, what is the most efficient way for the government to transfer public assets to private firms? What should the sale prices be for those assets? What role, if any, should the public sector have in the privatized system? How much time will be needed for effective competition to develop in privatized and deregulated transportation markets?

---

30. Relatively little scholarly empirical evidence exists on the effects of privatizing and deregulating taxis, intercity rail, and ports. Moore and Balaker (2006) conclude that taxi deregulation in the United States can benefit travelers if it is fully implemented. Barrett (2010) summarizes the evidence that taxi deregulation in Ireland generated significant benefits. Intercity passenger rail, Amtrak, is corporatized but constrained to serve unprofitable routes. Amtrak would clearly be more profitable if it were more cost efficient and free to choose which routes to serve and to set prices for those routes. Eliminating Amtrak's subsidies would also encourage it to provide better service. Competition among private ports appears to be workable, as suggested by the fact that most large port facilities in the United Kingdom are private. In the United States privatized ports in San Pedro and Long Beach, California, could, for example, compete with each other for traffic. However, to the best of my knowledge, the issue has not been studied.

Should regulations be implemented during the transition to effective competition? What contingency plans should be developed in the event that privatization results in a financial collapse of a significant part of the system or in a monopoly provider that faces no competitive discipline?

The motivation for privatization is clear, and its potential to improve upon public provision has some evidentiary support. But given that important uncertainties about privatization's economic effects remain and that enormous stakes are involved, I proceed in the next chapter to outline experiments that are essential for understanding privatization's likely economic effects and for strengthening its case with the public.

9

Privatization Experiments

A major policy reform can occur if policymakers are convinced that it will have its intended effects and that constituents, especially influential ones, will benefit. Experiments are invaluable for providing policymakers with evidence that can be used to justify and guide policy reforms. For example, the European Union has been able to learn from a variety of policy experiments conducted by its member countries. Similarly, the size and diversity of the United States facilitates such experiments before policymakers have to decide whether to implement a policy nationwide.

I do not expect policymakers to run controlled experiments; rather, in the context of transportation privatization and deregulation, experiments would consist of policymakers identifying certain markets and giving firms in those markets the freedom to innovate and compete. Policymakers would then respond accordingly to the results. For example, the California and Texas intrastate airline "deregulation experiments" helped convince policymakers to support deregulation of the U.S. airline industry by showing that, controlling for flight distance, fares on highly regulated interstate routes greatly exceeded those on largely unregulated intrastate routes (Breyer 1982). However, airline deregulation could not succeed politically without a supplemental policy to assuage congressional fears that small communities would lose airline service, so Congress enacted the Essential Air Services program. At the same time, as Kahn (1989) points out, policymakers failed to heed warnings that airline deregulation's economic performance would be compromised unless the Federal Aviation Administration (FAA) took steps to implement airport congestion pricing to reduce the expected increase in peak-period traffic.

Government's effort in previous centuries to shift most of the provision of transportation from the private to the public sector does not indicate that privatization cannot succeed today because much of the financial collapse that preceded government intervention was attributable to government regulations that undermined private operators' performance. Most private companies were in the early stages of developing their networks and operations; hence regulations that inhibited such development greatly hurt profitability.

The inefficient practices that have existed for decades in the nation's transportation system must be purged and the system's technology must be upgraded. Private firms are more likely to succeed in accomplishing those goals than they were in developing the nation's transportation system while being undermined by intrusive government regulations. As noted, the public-private partnerships that have been established for a very small set of projects in the country are not designed to showcase the benefits of a full-fledged privatization program, although they do indicate that the nation is gradually accepting the idea of greater private sector involvement in the transportation system and that the private sector is capable of financing and managing large-scale transportation investments.[1]

It is useful for policymakers to have some broad a priori expectations of privatization's economic effects to guide their assessments of the experimental evidence, so I first summarize the inefficiencies of the U.S. transportation system that have been discussed previously—and in many cases quantified—and briefly discuss the potential for privatization to reduce them. To be sure, surprises will exist—as they surely did for airline deregulation (Kahn 1988)—and neither I nor policymakers nor anyone else will be able to anticipate many of them. Acknowledging the existence of surprises underscores the importance of experiments to help policymakers implement privatization and deregulation carefully. I then identify some conditions that would enhance the feasibility of experiments and their likelihood of economic and political success. Further guidance on conducting experiments should

---

1. There is also evidence in specific locales that the public may be starting to see the virtues in private sector solutions to infrastructure problems. For example, Mallory Simon, "Island DIY: Kauai Residents Don't Wait for State to Repair Road," *CNN.com,* April 9, 2009, reports that residents and businesses in Kauai, Hawaii, pulled together to repair an access road on their own in a matter of weeks because it would have taken years for state money to funnel in and for the state to complete the job. Jason Armstrong, "Do-It-Yourself Road Repair Advances," *West Hawaii Today,* April 8, 2010, describes a proposal where Hawaii County would provide free gravel, cinder, and other materials to residents so they can fix their rural roads. Lynh Bui, "South Scottsdale May Get Boost from New Law," *Arizona Republic,* May 21, 2010, reports that under a new law businesses in Scottsdale, Arizona, can pay for public infrastructure improvements through bonds backed by self-imposed property taxes.

emerge from comprehensive and intensive discussions between government officials, private analysts, academics, transportation providers, and transportation users, all of whom should be willing to share their knowledge and experience with how the system operates and the ways it can be improved to ensure that the transportation experiments provide accurate information about the likely effects of privatization.

Expected Effects of Privatization

Given the available empirical evidence, I have focused my assessment on highways, urban bus and rail transit, airports, and air traffic control. Table 9-1 summarizes the inefficiencies attributable to current public policies that have been reported in previous tables, includes estimates of their welfare costs where available, and speculates about privatization's effect on each source of inefficiency.

The sources of inefficiencies for each service form a recurrent theme of mispricing, misallocated funds, suboptimal service and investment, and inflated production costs. Collectively, they amount to more than $100 billion (2005 dollars) in annual welfare losses and motivate interest in fundamental institutional change.

I stress that I have not quantified the potentially large cost of slow technological advance. Major innovations such as the internal combustion engine, jet aircraft, and electric-powered trains have benefited consumers and firms during the past century by significantly increasing the speed and reducing the cost of transportation. But since the 1960s, during which time the public sector has continued to strongly affect the entire transportation sector, such innovations have not occurred. And although many recent advances in information technology have been adopted by the partially deregulated intercity modes, the benefits of those advances such as GPS applications in highways and transit operations have been left largely untapped in urban transportation.

One important exception is the continual technological advance in the comfort, performance, and safety of the private automobile. Indeed, the evolution of cars and light trucks with little improvement in the road itself shows how private sector competition spurs technical change. Public ownership of roads has, in fact, stymied innovations in the private auto because public roads do not communicate with vehicles in ways that would, for example, enable improvements in traffic flow by changing signal times when north-south traffic becomes much heavier than east-west traffic. Airlines do

Table 9-1. *Potential Improvements in Transportation Efficiency from Privatization*
2005 $

Transportation service	Current inefficiency	Welfare cost compared with optimal policy	Potential effect of privatization
Highways	Motorists and truckers are not efficiently charged for their contribution to congestion, resulting in travel delays, losses to shippers, and urban sprawl.	The failure to adopt efficient congestion pricing generates an annual welfare cost of $45 billion.[a]	The effects of privatization depend on the competitive environment. A monopoly provider could set excessive user charges. But allowing bargaining could moderate price increases and increase price-service options for road users. Regulation may also prevent excessive charges.
	Truckers are not efficiently charged for their contribution to pavement damage and bridge wear.	The failure to adopt efficient pavement-wear pricing for truckers generates an annual welfare cost of $10.8 billion.[b] No estimate is available for the welfare cost caused by the failure to adopt efficient pricing for bridge wear.	Owners of private highways would have an incentive to charge truckers for pavement damage and bridge wear to reduce costs. Bargaining could moderate excessive charges and give truckers an incentive to shift to vehicle axle configurations and loads that reduce their effect on the physical deterioration of the system.
	Road pavements are not built to minimize the sum of maintenance and capital costs and therefore require excessive maintenance expenditures.	The failure to build roads to optimal thickness results in an annual welfare cost of $12.5 billion.[c] Bridge design may also be suboptimal; but no estimate of the welfare cost is available.	Owners of private highways would have an economic incentive to minimize costs by building highways to optimal thickness.

Funds for highway projects are allocated among and within states based on a formula that does not explicitly seek to minimize highway costs.	The failure to allocate funds to minimize highway costs increases annual highway costs by $13.8 billion.[d]	Private highway firms would make investments to maximize profits and would not be constrained on where they allocate funds.
Regulations on labor increase the cost of building and maintaining highways.	The cost of Davis-Bacon regulations on hiring labor are some $680 million.[e] Labor regulations at the state level also raise costs.	Private highway firms would seek to minimize the cost of production and would not be bound by Davis-Bacon and state-level labor regulations.
Production costs are inflated from cost overruns that are attributable to the bidding process that selects the lowest-cost bidder.	Not available.	Private firms would not be subjected to the current bidding process and would seek to minimize costs in their negotiations with contractors.
A portion of highway revenues from the fuel tax are used to subsidize transit service.	No estimate is available. But given transit's questionable social desirability, the transfers are wasteful.	Private highways would not provide inefficient subsidies to transit.
Inefficient technology is used to construct pavement, which reduces pavement life and damages motorists' vehicles.	In California the annual welfare cost of using inferior methods to lay asphalt is roughly $1 billion.[f] An estimate of the welfare cost for other states is not available.	Private firms would have an incentive to use the most efficient road pavement technologies available and to encourage and adopt improvements in those technologies.
Toll booths are used to set and collect tolls on many highways. They contribute to congestion and make it costly and difficult to implement efficient road pricing.	No estimate is available. Former U.S. Department of Transportation secretary Peters has indicated the problem is serious and called for replacing all toll booths in the United States with all-electronic toll collection.	Private firms would have an incentive to use the most efficient road-pricing technologies available and to encourage and adopt improvements in those technologies.

(continued)

Table 9-1 (continued)

Transportation service	Current inefficiency	Welfare cost compared with optimal policy	Potential effect of privatization
	Incentives do not exist for public authorities to develop and implement new innovations that would improve highway travel.	Unknown but it is likely to be large given the potential for computer and satellite markets to improve highway travel.	Private firms would have an incentive to use the most efficient road technologies available and to encourage and adopt new technologies.
Urban transit	Transit fares are set well below marginal cost and, in fact, certain commuters ride free of charge.	The failure to set marginal cost fares for urban bus and rail travel produces an annual welfare loss of $3.6 billion.[g] No estimate is available for the welfare cost of programs that enable certain commuters—mainly federal government employees—to ride free of charge or to obtain a tax deduction for using transit.	Private transit firms would not subsidize users but seek to maximize profits. The effects of privatization depend on the extent of competition. Intermodal competition would limit excessive charges.
	Bus and rail transit frequency is excessive, and route coverage fails to keep up with demographic changes.	Transit's failure to set optimal frequencies and charge marginal-cost fares produces an annual welfare loss of $10.6 billion.[h] No estimate is available for the welfare cost of suboptimal route coverage.	Private transit firms would provide route coverage and frequency to maximize profits. Niche carriers could enter and potentially fill in any gaps in coverage.
	Transit is prevented from providing other services such as charter services and opening and developing retail shops near transit stations.	No estimate is available.	Private transit carriers would exploit economies of scope in transport service and possibly benefit from operating retail outlets.

	Many transit projects have gone forward because costs have been underestimated and ridership overestimated.	The average cost escalation for rail projects has been estimated to be as high as 40 percent.[i] In the process, socially undesirable systems are built. The annual welfare cost of socially undesirable urban rail systems approaches $5 billion; the cost of socially undesirable urban bus systems is $8.6 billion.[j]	In a privatized environment, some socially undesirable systems may be abandoned while new systems would be developed if they were privately profitable.
	Regulations such as "buy American" provisions, capital subsidies, Section 13(c) restrictions on releasing an employee, and the like inflate the cost of transit service. In addition, standardized vehicle sizes inflate costs by contributing to excess capacity.	No estimate is available of the aggregate cost of inefficient operations. But these costs are reflected in estimates that indicate a sharp decline in transit labor productivity.[k]	Private transit firms would have an incentive to minimize costs and to align vehicle sizes with demand.
	Up-to-date technologies such as in the field of telematics are not used to improve service and attract riders. And new innovations are not developed.	Unknown, but it is likely to be large given the potential that exists to improve transit operations.	Private firms would have an incentive to use the most efficient transit technologies available and to encourage and adopt new technologies.
Airports	Aircraft are not charged for their contribution to delays, thus increasing travelers' delay costs and airlines' operating costs.	The failure to set efficient takeoff and landing tolls results in an annual welfare loss of roughly $6 billion.[l]	The effect of privatization depends on the competitive environment that evolves. Allowing bargaining could moderate price increases.
	Airports have instituted slot controls to limit operations, but those reduce competition and raise fares.	Slot controls have resulted in an aggregate annual increase in fares of $0.72 billion on routes involving New York LaGuardia and Chicago O'Hare.[m]	Private airports would eliminate slot controls and use prices to ration the available runway capacity.

(continued)

Table 9-1 (*continued*)

Transportation service	Current inefficiency	Welfare cost compared with optimal policy	Potential effect of privatization
	Regulatory hurdles increase the time and cost to build new runways and extend existing runways.	The failure of airports to build optimal runway capacity and set efficient runway charges produces an annual welfare loss of $16 billion.[n]	Private airports would be more aggressive than public airports are at trying to overcome regulatory hurdles to expanding capacity.
	The limited availability of gates reduces competition and raises fares.	The annual aggregate increase in fares attributable to the limited availability of gates at many major and midsize airports is $4.4 billion.[o]	Private airports would seek to attract airlines to maximize profits and enable any carrier to enter that was willing to pay the cost of service and terminal facilities.
	Screening for passenger security could be implemented at much lower cost and enable travelers to incur much shorter delays without sacrificing the security benefits provided.	No estimate is available, especially because it is difficult to determine the optimal level of security.	Private airports would search for the most efficient way to provide airport security by assessing public and private providers and encouraging innovations in security technology that they would implement in a timely manner.
Air traffic control (ATC)	Aircraft are undercharged for their contribution to congestion in airspace around airports, which increases travelers' delay costs and airlines' operating costs.	No estimate available.	A private ATC system would be responsive to users' preferences and would determine price-service packages through negotiations with users.

Funds for ATC facilities are not allocated to minimize delay costs, thus increasing the costs of the system and forcing users to incur higher delay costs.	The failure to allocate funds to towers and TRACONs to minimize costs is responsible for an annual welfare cost of more than $1.13 billion.[p]	A private ATC system would have an incentive to allocate its funds in the most efficient way possible.
New technologies are not adopted in an efficient, expeditious manner, thus increasing the costs of the system and preventing users from lowering delay costs.	Although billions of dollars have arguably been wasted, no empirical estimate is available because of the difficulty of determining the cost-minimizing adoption policy.	A private ATC system would have the incentive and freedom to adopt and implement the latest technologies and to encourage suppliers to develop new technologies.

a. Langer and Winston (2008).
b. Small, Winston, and Evans (1989).
c. Small, Winston, and Evans (1989).
d. Winston and Langer (2006).
e. Allen (1983).
f. Gillen (2001).
g. Winston and Shirley (1998).
h. Winston and Shirley (1998).
i. Flyvbjerg, Holm, and Buhl (2002).
j. Winston and Maheshri (2007), Winston and Shirley (2006).
k. Lave (1991).
l. Morrison and Winston (1989).
m. Morrison and Winston (2000).
n. Morrison and Winston (1989).
o. Morrison and Winston (2000).
p. Morrison and Winston (2008).

"communicate" with their infrastructure; but, as noted, their communication could be greatly improved.[2]

Table 9-1 indicates that privatization offers firms the incentive and opportunity to reduce production costs, make efficient investments, improve service quality, and accelerate technological change. In the process large public subsidies would also be eliminated.

I have suggested that in certain services and markets valid concerns exist that private firms would be able to set excessive charges and dramatically cut service because they face little competition or that they might experience serious financial difficulties. Unfortunately, evidence is not available to allow me to speculate with great confidence about whether intense competition could be supplied by firms providing the same service, by alternative modes, and by consumers through negotiations as an organized bargaining unit; whether users could own stock in a company that owns their transportation infrastructure and thus have some control over corporate policy and possibly benefit if the value of the company appreciates; and whether private firms could earn sufficient profits to maintain transportation services and infrastructure and make investments that respond to users' preferences for new services and facilities.

Generally, it is reasonable to suggest that urban transit would operate in a highly competitive environment and face modest demand and that highways, airports, and air traffic control would operate in an imperfectly competitive—possibly even monopolistic—environment and face strong demand. Beyond those broad classifications, experiments are necessary to provide quantitative evidence on the intensity of various potential sources of competition, the strength of demand in the long run, firms' long-run financial performance, and the evolution of capital markets in a deregulated and privatized transportation environment in the United States.

---

2. Robert Poole, *ATC Reform News* (Los Angeles: Reason Foundation, January 2010), includes commentary by R. Michael Baiada, who argues that air travel delays could be significantly reduced if arrival queues could be moved forward—that is, if several airlines are scheduled to land at 8 a.m. and runway capacity is available before then, air traffic control and the airlines should try to have certain aircraft arrive before 8 a.m. The general point is that greater efforts should be made to use the available runway and airspace capacity throughout the day. I would argue that such efforts are not made today because airports and air traffic control do not encourage efficient capacity utilization; but such efforts would be made by privatized aviation infrastructure providers because they and their customers—namely, the airlines—would have an economic incentive to work together to reduce delays and operating costs and to increase throughput.

Basic Considerations in Motivating and Designing Experiments

Congressional legislation for airports and highways has included funding and tax breaks to explore privatization to a limited extent, so the idea of transportation privatization experiments in the United States is not new.[3] But before widespread experimentation can occur, formidable political, institutional, and legal issues must be addressed. Thus, in general, the federal government will have to make the case to the public for why transportation experiments are of great importance and, if necessary, will have to provide incentives for states and localities to join the effort.

As noted, deregulation of intercity transportation was "sold" by its political proponents as a policy to reduce consumer prices during a decade of high inflation. Policymakers were therefore able to create a sense of urgency to enlist public support and overcome the objections of powerful interest groups, such as organized labor, by seizing on the national deregulatory movement at the time (Robyn 1987).

A similar approach could be taken to gain public support for privatization and deregulation of the transportation system. All levels of government are facing enormous fiscal pressures for the foreseeable future as a result of the deep recession that began in late 2007. The public hardly needs to be convinced that funding may not be available to keep the transportation system from significantly deteriorating and greatly affecting the quality of life, especially following such recent major disruptions as the fatal crash between two Washington, D.C., Metro trains and the closing of the Oakland Bay Bridge for several weeks. Governments can vastly improve their budgetary situation by selling transportation services and infrastructure to private firms and giving them the opportunity to attract additional capital.

In addition, as the economy recovers from the recession, privatization and deregulation could facilitate important sources of economic growth. First, technological advance in transportation is more likely to occur in the private sector than it has in the public sector. Second, while privatization would cause labor to be used more efficiently and eliminate certain positions

3. In 1996 Congress enacted legislation creating an airport privatization pilot program, but a city or state had to obtain the approval of airlines representing 65 percent of the landed weight at the airport. In the case of roads, the Transportation Infrastructure Finance and Innovation Act of 1998 established a new federal credit program under which the U.S. Department of Transportation may provide a private highway firm with taxpayer subsidized credit. As part of the 2005 Safe, Accountable, Flexible, Efficient Transportation Equity Act, state agencies that work with private highway firms may issue tax-exempt bonds on behalf of the project.

that exist in the public sector, it also would spur the creation of young firms that are a vital force for job creation (Haltiwanger, Jarmin, and Miranda 2010). Third, as noted in the introduction, parts of the transportation sector have historically attracted some of the finest business leaders in the nation. Privatization would give the entire sector the opportunity to attract exceptional innovative leaders who could fully use their skills in new enterprises. Finally, it is noteworthy that Warren Buffett has recently made a large investment in Burlington Northern–Santa Fe railroad—something he certainly did not do when the industry was regulated. It is likely that privatization and deregulation of the U.S. transportation system would create new investment opportunities that attract significant investments from firms and individuals throughout the world.

The status quo is not a viable option because budgets are unlikely to improve in the near future, while congestion, delays, potential threats to safety, and the like will only become worse. In sum, broad public interest in privatization and deregulation of the transportation system can be generated by arguing that such a policy is necessary to ameliorate the nation's fiscal problems and to promote economic growth. The evidence obtained from experiments would then, I hope, indicate that individual citizens will benefit from the policy's effects on the transportation system. Attracting the support of the broad public will be essential for overcoming objections of special interests who perceive they may lose the rents they receive from the current system.

Leading up to the experiments, the federal government should take preliminary steps to show how government's role in the transportation system will be substantially reduced. As Roth (2005) observes, Congress, in passing the 1956 Highway Act, envisioned that its obligation to finance road projects would end in 1972 with the completion of the Interstate Highway System. The federal government should, at long last, cease to be a source of highway finance and encourage state and local governments—which would be solely responsible for highways—to explore privatization experiments. It should also stop supporting construction of new transit systems and costly extensions of existing ones. Finally, although commercial airports are owned by local municipalities and sometimes by states, they receive federal airport development grants, have access to federal tax-exempt financing, and are subject to federal regulatory control. The federal government should end its role in financing and regulating commercial airports.

Careful thought should go into identifying contexts that would enhance the political appeal of transportation privatization experiments. Table 9-2 frames experiments for each service and facility by noting specific factors

Table 9-2. *Contexts for Transportation Experiments*

Transportation experiment	Motivating factors	Location	Potential benefits
Highways	Significant delays, crumbling infrastructure, state and city budgetary crises	Undermaintained highway corridor(s) in congested metropolitan area that is unlikely to receive substantial government funding	Motorists' travel time and reliability improve, tolling is flexible and responsive to users' preferences, and gasoline tax is rebated to road users
Bus and rail transit	Deteriorating system and concerns about safety; major funding shortfalls	System running a large deficit in a city where a notable share of the population uses the system	Improve the convenience and reliability of transit, use up-to-date information technology, optimize vehicle sizes, and expand services
Airports	Significant delays	Congested airport that is not receiving major federal funding to expand capacity	Reduce travelers' delay and carriers' operating costs, and increase carrier competition
Air traffic control	Significant delays	Major U.S. air travel corridor	Improve travel speeds and reduce carriers' operating costs

that motivate the experiments, key features of a location where the benefits from privatization are most likely to be realized, and potential benefits to travelers and carriers.

Highways

The government should focus on a metropolitan area with little likelihood of substantial state or local government funding and with congested and deteriorating roads whose performance may improve significantly if they are privatized. To conduct a privatization experiment, the government must select a corridor to transfer to the private sector, a private entity (or entities) must express interest in acquiring the road, the terms of sale must be determined, and the private operator(s) must be able to generate revenues to finance its investment.

Several well-financed global infrastructure companies are likely to have an interest in purchasing a U.S. urban highway that is for sale, either alone or, to avoid protectionist objections, as part of a joint venture with a U.S. infrastructure firm. The transaction should be a sale, not a lease, and the government should not set an excessive sale price because that would affect the tolls set by the private provider and reduce travelers' welfare (Winston and Yan 2010). A poorly designed privatization experiment could result in the road quickly reverting back to the public sector and discourage other cities from embarking on similar experiments. Engel, Fischer, and Galetovic (2003, 2006) have pointed out that flawed franchise contracts have undermined the benefits from public-private partnerships in the United States and in Latin America.

The sale should not include regulations that undermine the private firm's ability to set tolls to operate the road and to earn a return on its investment. But given that the transaction is a long-run experiment, the government should make clear that as the experiment evolves, the government may learn that the benefits from privatization could be enhanced if it introduces appropriate supplemental policies. In addition, the government should allow organizations to form with the purpose of representing motorists, truckers, and government services in negotiations with the private highway operator over toll schedules.[4] Private highway operators would be prohibited from forming such organizations to avoid the potential for colluding on tolls. Finally, electronic tolling would enable motorists to keep track of their mileage on the private road and to receive an accurate rebate for the gasoline taxes that they incur from using it.

Urban Transit

Local governments facing deteriorating bus service and funding shortfalls could develop privatization experiments by allowing a private bus company to make its own decisions about fares, frequency, route coverage, vehicle sizes, and the like without imposing any regulations on its operations. City officials should also indicate that as part of the experiment, private vans and jitneys along with taxis would be allowed to compete in a privatized and deregulated urban transit environment.[5]

---

4. Truckers have expressed interest in truck-only toll roads (Samuel, Poole, and Holguin-Veras 2002). Such facilities could also be included as part of the highway privatization experiment. A private firm could be given the opportunity to build and operate a truck-only road and negotiate prices and service with all segments of the trucking industry.

5. As noted, certain cities have already deregulated taxi service. Private firms occasionally provide van or jitney service for their employees or customers, but commercial service is generally not considered to be a component of the current urban transit system.

A local government should complete the experiment by privatizing its rail transit system, if one exists. Consideration should be given to selling different rail lines on a system to different private operators to facilitate intramodal competition and, as the experiment evolves, to allow efficient firms to supplant less efficient firms. In addition, private rail transit firms should be given the opportunity to improve their finances by developing the surrounding property near their stations for commercial purposes.[6] In sum, the goal of the urban transit experiment should be to allow private rail, buses, vans, jitneys, and taxis to engage with the private automobile in unfettered price and service-quality competition for travelers.

Airports

U.S. airport competition already exists to some extent as airports located in adjacent metropolitan areas compete for passengers through their location and the airlines that serve them. However, congested airports do not attempt to enhance their competitive position by reforming pricing policies to reduce delays. Privatization experiments would eliminate current restrictions on airport price and service offerings and give congested airports an incentive to compete for passengers and carriers by efficiently producing a level of service valued by users.

The existing airport privatization program passed by Congress should be extended to allow local and state governments to sell airports in the same and adjacent metropolitan areas to different private owners. As part of the experiment, private airports that are currently prevented from offering commercial scheduled service should be allowed to do so. The appropriate government authority would determine an airport's sales price with a private buyer, but the authority would be prohibited from imposing residual regulations as a condition of a sale. Similar to highway privatization experiments, the authority should allow organizations to form with the purpose of representing commercial air carriers, business jets, and general aviation in negotiations with private airports over toll schedules. Private airports would be expected to finance themselves with takeoff and landing tolls, parking fees, and concession rents and without tax-exempt debt financing. As noted, concession rents could be determined in a more competitive environment by selling the airfield and the airport terminals to different owners.

---

6. Because one of the goals of privatization is to wean transit systems off public subsidies, it would be inadvisable to subsidize rail firms' nontransportation commercial ventures.

Air Traffic Control

The creation of the NextGen (Next Generation) air traffic control system, a collection of ongoing and new programs that are intended to triple air space capacity by 2025 by replacing radar with satellite technology, was announced by the federal government in 2004. A good opportunity to conduct a privatization experiment for the air traffic control system may, in fact, be while it is in transition. Indeed, Robyn (2007) has identified some important steps that the FAA can take to make NextGen a market-oriented system.

NextGen could respond to the preferences of airspace users by developing improvements in specific regions of the country that users are willing to pay for. For example, Nav Canada is installing ADS-B (Automatic Dependent Surveillance-Broadcast) from the global satellite network over the Hudson Bay, which is not served by radar, because international flights are willing to pay for real-time weather information that reduces aircraft separation and delays. Generally, user fees could facilitate mutually beneficial business decisions that providers and users are likely to make on a regular basis.

In addition, the federal government should encourage airports to assume appropriate responsibility for terminal-area NextGen infrastructure by modifying their current Rates and Charges Policy. The FAA should allow private firms to perform functions that are not inherently governmental and, by implementing sophisticated NextGen technology, could allow aircraft to experiment with self-separation.

As the system evolves, the federal government should explore ways to privatize NextGen while devising incentives, perhaps through contracts, to make it fully accountable to aircraft operators and other stakeholders. As Robyn (2007) discusses, a privatized organization could be charged with developing and deploying the components of the system and be allowed to impose user charges and borrow money in the capital market. At the same time, NextGen could be placed under the control of a stakeholder board with its own, independent staff. Such a board would, among other things, ensure that expenditures on the system were justified by their benefits.[7]

The Role of the Public Sector

Experiments would provide an opportunity for stakeholders to assess the potential benefits of privatization and for policymakers to consider carefully

---

7. Privatization experiments could also be designed and conducted for intercity passenger rail service on a selected corridor, such as the Northeast corridor, and for ports in a specific coastal region, such as Southern California.

if they could enhance those benefits. Ideally, the experiments would succeed without government intervention, but that is unlikely politically and possibly economically. Policymakers may insist on certain supplemental policies or regulations before they are willing to undertake privatization experiments and, as in the case of intercity transportation deregulation, before they support privatization legislation.

Once implemented, the experiments should be viewed as a long-term learning process. Accordingly participants and observers must be patient and flexible in how they allow the experiments to evolve to generate data that will greatly inform policymaking. Some experiments, such as highway privatization, are likely to take longer to develop and involve more risk than, say, bus privatization. In the case of highway privatization, I prefer selling the existing lanes to a single firm, which would negotiate with a third party to determine tolls. But in the long run, experiments may indicate that the toll-negotiating process provides modest discipline on a private operator's market power and that user benefits could be enhanced if the government sold the road's capacity to two competing firms.

Armstrong and Sappington (2006) point out that even if an industry is privatized, regulation may still be appropriate. But they also indicate that regulations often induce inefficient performance and that competition is likely to be a more effective "regulator." In the context I outline here, the government's judgment would be critical because a private firm's behavior will evolve as technology and the market evolves, and experiments may reveal that privatization and deregulation initially produce static inefficiencies, which eventually diminish as the private firm sheds the public sector's capital structure and becomes more efficient over time. Regulation may have adverse consequences for privatization's long-run performance or, if designed effectively, could allow privatization to move forward because it has addressed the concerns of influential opponents and may have enabled—or at least appeared to have enabled—certain constituents to benefit from the policy.[8]

Government has an important role in ensuring that a privatized and deregulated transportation system satisfies the nation's environmental and safety

8. For example, I pointed out that road users could gain from privatization if they were represented by a third party who negotiated tolls with a private operator. In practice, the negotiations may not result in a gain to road users unless they are supplemented by "price cap" regulations. Generally, policymakers' potential interventions should be a carefully nuanced part of privatization experiments so that private firms are not given incentives to "game" the system. The threat of supplemental price regulation, for instance, may cause a private firm to inhibit its market power in the short run and give observers a distorted sense of the intensity of competition in the privatized environment.

objectives.[9] Concerns about climate change are spurring ever greater interest in regulating carbon-based emissions from all transportation sources; hence government will have the challenging responsibility of designing efficient carbon dioxide charges without unduly compromising transportation suppliers and users. In fact, technologies that make it easier for private authorities to implement road pricing and air traffic control charges—because they monitor users' behavior and its effects in real time—may also make it easier for these private authorities to implement efficient vehicle and aircraft emission charges. Intercity transportation safety has continued to improve under deregulation, but a definitive causal relationship has not been established. Although policymakers will undoubtedly maintain the existing safety regulation functions of the various transportation agencies, the benefit of those regulations should be reassessed given that privatized firms' facilities and services are likely to become safer as they adopt safety-enhancing technologies.

Summary

The available scholarly evidence suggests that privatization and deregulation of the U.S. transportation system could improve the efficiency of firms' operations and technology but does not resolve whether competition would be sufficiently intense and whether private operators would be financially stable over the long run to enable travelers to benefit from the policy reform. Given this critical uncertainty and others, the case for privatization and deregulation must include supportive evidence from experiments conducted in the United States. The experiments should be designed to ensure that effective competition can develop, while observers should accept that private firms will need considerable time to replace the public sector's capital structure with their own, more efficient capital structure. As experiments evolve, analysts should assess their economic outcomes and, if necessary, devise supplemental government policies that could enhance the transportation system's performance in a privatized environment.

---

9. It is worth noting that even in the area of traffic safety, Makowsky and Stratmann (2009) conclude that political forces play a role because police officers will consider their local government's fiscal condition and the driver's ability to vote in local elections when deciding whether to issue a fine.

10

Conclusion

The public sector's large role in the U.S. transportation system is attributable to economic shocks at various times in the nation's history that have left private providers of transportation service and infrastructure in financial ruin. But government regulations and the failure of policymakers to make constructive interventions also have played a significant role in the fate of private transportation firms. Until the late 1970s the nation's transportation system consisted of intercity modes that were heavily regulated; urban modes that, with the exception of the automobile, were owned and operated by the public sector; and infrastructure that, with the exception of the intercity freight rail network, was owned and operated by the public sector.

The accumulated scholarly and anecdotal evidence indicates that government's extensive involvement in the U.S. transportation system has resulted in massive inefficiencies and slow technological advance. Deregulation of the intercity modes, which began in the late 1970s, was an important first step toward improving the efficiency of the system by reducing government's constraints on efficient operations and by stimulating carrier competition and technological advance.

In this book, I have explored the case for privatizing and deregulating most of the transportation system with the goal of creating workably competitive markets that would substantially improve the system's performance. The motivation for such dramatic institutional change is compelling given the state of the system, and the case for the recommended course of action toward the partially deregulated intercity transportation modes is strongly supported. But the case for privatizing and deregulating urban transit and public infrastructure has limited theoretical and empirical support. Because that conclusion does not enable me to meet Stigler's (1965) standard for credible economic policy advice—no economist should proffer a policy position without persuasive evidence of the economic effects of that policy— I have argued that experiments are necessary to reduce important uncertainties surrounding the effects of privatization and deregulation of highways, urban transit, and aviation infrastructure on the welfare of travelers, operators, and investors.

Policymakers, however, are currently focused on national fundraising strategies for infrastructure investments—particularly for highways—that include a National Infrastructure Bank, grants from the American Recovery and Reinvestment Act of 2009 (popularly known as the stimulus bill), and taxes on vehicle-miles traveled. As noted, $8 billion of stimulus funds has already been appropriated to expand high-speed rail service without conducting any serious economic analysis. Such spending would do little to address the vast inefficiencies in the system and would entail considerable waste. Moreover, efforts to increase public spending on transportation would "waste" the opportunity created by the current economic crisis to conduct privatization experiments that could lead to the adoption of a policy that would enable all levels of government to reduce their expenditures and raise revenues by selling certain assets that would become more productive in the private sector, thereby increasing the nation's welfare.

It has become abundantly clear that the weak incentive structure inherent in public sector activities makes government incapable of reforming the management and operations of the transportation system. The strong status quo bias that characterizes transportation policy and the system's shortcomings will produce even more frustrations in the years to come for travelers and shippers and place greater strains on public coffers. Delaying privatization experiments would add to the growing costs of inaction by making it even more difficult for new private firms to shed the public sector's accumulated inefficiencies.

In the current economic climate, policymakers and the public are especially justified for questioning whether the private market can improve the efficiency of the nation's transportation system, instead of contributing to a major crisis that creates havoc for travelers and shippers. Experiments represent a reasonable low-risk option that would enable policymakers to carefully explore whether privatization can create sufficiently competitive markets in transportation to greatly increase Americans' satisfaction with how they and their goods move throughout the country.

Moreover, experiments could lead to unlocking constraints that now hobble the development of a national technologically advanced transportation system. The traditional characterization of the system in terms of urban and intercity modes and infrastructure is the result of government regulation and ownership. Privatization could result in more integrated, intermodal, and multimodal service, thereby enabling, say, one firm to provide all segments of a trip abroad door to door. Perhaps a new revolutionary transportation technology may, at long last, emerge that would have been impeded by the public sector. Like travel itself, the potential of a privatized and deregulated system should be limited only by our imagination.

References

Advani, Asheesh. 1999. "Passenger-Friendly Airports: Another Reason for Airport Privatization." Policy Study 254. Los Angeles: Reason Foundation.

Albalate, Daniel, Germà Bel, and Xavier Fageda. 2007. "Privatization and Regulation of Toll Motorways in Europe." University of Barcelona, Research Institute of Applied Economics (March).

Allen, Steven G. 1983. "Much Ado about Davis-Bacon: A Critical Review and New Evidence." *Journal of Law and Economics* 26 (October): 707–36.

Altshuler, Alan, and David Luberoff. 2003. *Mega-Projects: The Changing Politics of Urban Public Investment.* Brookings.

Armstrong, Mark, and David E. M. Sappington. 2006. "Regulation, Competition, and Liberalization." *Journal of Economic Literature* 44 (June): 325–66.

Atkinson, Robert D., and Daniel D. Castro. 2008. *Digital Quality of Life: Understanding the Personal and Social Benefits of the Information Technology Revolution.* Washington: Information and Technology Foundation.

Bajari, Patrick, Stephanie Houghton, and Steve Tadellis. 2006. "Bidding for Incomplete Contracts: An Empirical Analysis." Working Paper 12051. Cambridge, Mass.: National Bureau of Economic Research (February).

Ball, Michael O., George Donohue, and Karla Hoffman. 2006. "Auctions for the Safe, Efficient and Equitable Allocation of Airspace System Resources." In *Combinatorial Auctions*, edited by Peter Cramton, Yoav Shoham, and Richard Steinberg. MIT Press.

Barrett, Sean. 2009. *Deregulation and the Airline Business in Europe: Selected Readings.* New York: Routledge.

Barrett, Sean D. 2010. "The Sustained Impacts of Taxi Deregulation." *Economic Affairs* 30 (March 11).

Barry, Phil. 2004. "Does Privatisation Work?" Policy Backgrounder 5. Wellington: New Zealand Business Roundtable (December).

Baum-Snow, Nathaniel, and Matthew Kahn. 2005. "The Effects of Urban Rail Transit Expansions: Evidence from Sixteen Cities, 1970 to 2000." *Brookings-Wharton Papers on Urban Affairs:* 1–60.

Bilotkach, Volodmyr, Joseph A. Clougherty, Juergen Mueller, and Anming Zhang. 2010. "Regulation, Privatization, and Aeronautical Charges: Panel Data Evidence from European Airports," Working Paper, University of California, Irvine, Department of Economics (June).

Bitzan, John D., and Theodore E. Keeler. 2007. "Economies of Density and Regulatory Change in the U.S. Railroad Freight Industry." *Journal of Law and Economics* 50 (February): 157–79.

Blalock, Garrick, Vrinda Kadiyali, and Daniel H. Simon. 2007. "The Impact of Post-9/11 Airport Security Measures on the Demand for Air Travel." *Journal of Law and Economics* 50 (November): 731–55.

Bollinger, Christopher, and Keith Ihlanfeldt. 1997. "The Impact of Rapid Rail Transit on Economic Development: The Case of Atlanta's MARTA." *Journal of Urban Economics* 42 (September): 179–204.

Borenstein, Severin, and Nancy L. Rose. 2007. "How Airline Markets Work . . . Or Do They? Regulatory Reform in the Airline Industry." Working Paper 13452. Cambridge, Mass: National Bureau of Economic Research (September).

Breyer, Stephen G. 1982. *Regulation and Its Reform.* Harvard University Press.

Brueckner, Jan K. 2002. "Airport Congestion When Carriers Have Market Power." *American Economic Review* 92 (December):1357–75.

———. 2003. "Airline Traffic and Urban Economic Development." *Urban Studies* 40: 1455–69.

Burch, Philip H. 1962. *Highway Revenue and Expenditure Policy in the United States.* Rutgers University Press.

BTS (Bureau of Transportation Statistics). 2006. *Condition of U.S. Road Bridges by State, 2006.* U.S. Department of Transportation.

Calcott, Paul, and Shuntian Yao. 2005. "Competition between Highway Operators: Can We Expect Toll Differentiation?" *Papers in Regional Science* 84 (November): 615–26.

Calfee, John, and Clifford Winston. 1998. "The Value of Automobile Travel Time: Implications for Congestion Policy." *Journal of Public Economics* 69 (July): 83–102.

Carlin, Alan, and R. E. Park. 1970. "Marginal Cost Pricing of Airport Runway Capacity." *American Economic Review* 60 (June): 310–19.

CBO (Congressional Budget Office). 1992. *Paying for Highways, Airways, and Waterways: How Can Users Be Charged?* Washington.

Charles, John. 2001. "The Mythical World of Transit Oriented Development." Policy Perspective 1019. Portland, Ore.: Cascade Policy Institute (October).

Coase, Ronald. 1972. "Durability and Monopoly." *Journal of Law and Economics* 15 (April): 143–49.

Cromwell, Brian. 1991. "Public Sector Maintenance: The Case of Local Mass Transit." *National Tax Journal* 44 (June): 199–212.

Currie, Janet, and Reed Walker. 2009. "Traffic Congestion and Infant Health: Evidence from E-Zpass." Working Paper 15413. Cambridge, Mass.: National Bureau of Economic Research (October).

Daniel, Joseph I. 1995. "Congestion Pricing and Capacity of Large Hub Airports: A Bottleneck Model with Stochastic Queues." *Econometrica* 63 (March): 327–70.

Denison, Edward F. 1985. *Trends in American Economic Growth, 1929–1982.* Brookings.

de Palma, Andre, and Robin Lindsey. 2000. "Private Toll Roads: Competition under Various Ownership Regimes." *Annals of Regional Science* 34 (March): 13–35.

———. 2002. "Private Roads, Competition, and Incentives to Adopt Time-Based Congestion Tolling." *Journal of Urban Economics* 52 (September): 217–41.

Derthick, Martha, and Paul J. Quirk. 1985. *The Politics of Deregulation.* Brookings.

Dewatripont, Mathias, and Patrick Legros. 2005. "Public-Private-Partnerships: Contract Design and Risk Transfer." EIB Papers 10:120–145. Luxembourg: European Investment Bank.

Dilger, Robert Jay. 2003. *American Transportation Policy.* Westport, Conn.: Praeger.

———. 2009. *Federalism Issues in Surface Transportation Policy: Past and Present.* Congressional Research Service, March.

Dillingham, Gerald. 2003. "Air Traffic Control, FAA's Modernization Efforts—Past, Present, and Future." Statement before the Subcommittee on Aviation, Committee on Transportation and Infrastructure, U.S. House of Representatives, October 30, 2003 (GAO-04-227T).

Duranton, Gilles, and Matthew A. Turner. 2008. "Urban Growth and Transportation." Working Paper. University of Toronto, Department of Economics.

Edelson, Noel M. 1971. "Congestion Tolls under Monopoly." *American Economic Review* 61 (December): 873–82.

Engel, Eduardo M., Ronald Fischer, and Alexander Galetovic. 2003. "Privatizing Highways in Latin America: Fixing What Went Wrong." *Economía* 4: 129–58.

———. 2006. "Privatizing Highways in the United States." *Review of Industrial Organization* 29, no. 1: 27–53.

———. 2007. "The Basic Public Finance of Public-Private Partnerships." Working Paper 13284. Cambridge, Mass.: National Bureau of Economic Research (October).

Evans, Diana. 1994. "Policy and Pork: The Use of Pork Barrel Projects to Build Policy Coalitions in the House of Representatives." *American Journal of Political Science* 38 (November): 894–917.

Finkelstein, Amy. 2009. "EZ Tax: Tax Salience and Tax Rates." *Quarterly Journal of Economics* 124 (August): 969–1010.

Flyvbjerg, Bent, Mette K. Skamris Holm, and Soren L. Buhl. 2002. "Underestimating Costs in Public Works Projects: Error or Lie?" *Journal of the American Planning Association* 68 (Summer): 279–95.

Forsyth, Peter. 2008. "Airport Policy in Australia and New Zealand: Privatization, Light-Handed Regulation, and Performance." In *Aviation Infrastructure Performance: A Study in Comparative Political Economy*, edited by Clifford Winston and Gines de Rus, pp. 65–99. Brookings.

Fox, Nancy Ruth, and Lawrence J. White. 1997. "U.S. Ocean Shipping Policy: Going against the Tide." *Annals of the American Academy of Political and Social Science* 553 (September): 75–86.

Friedman, Milton, and Daniel Boorstin. 1951. "How to Plan and Pay for the Safe and Adequate Highways We Need." Epilogue in *Roads in a Market Economy* (2006), edited by Gabriel J. Roth, pp. 223–45. Aldershot, U.K.: Avebury Technical.

Gallamore, Robert E. 1999. "Regulation and Innovation: Lessons from the American Railroad Industry." In *Essays in Transportation Economics and Policy: A Handbook in Honor of John R. Meyer*, edited by Jose A. Gomez-Ibanez, William B. Tye, and Clifford Winston, pp. 493–529. Brookings.

GAO (United States General Accounting Office). 1992. *Surface Transportation: Availability of Intercity Bus Service Continues to Decline.* GAO/RECD-92-126 (June).

———. 1996. *Urban Transportation: Metropolitan Planning Organizations' Efforts to Meet Federal Planning Requirements.* GAO/ RECD-96-200 (September).

———. 1998. *Air Traffic Control: Status of FAA's Modernization Program.* GAO/ RCED-99-25 (December).

———. 1999a. *Air Traffic Control: FAA's Modernization Investment Management Approach Could Be Strengthened.* GAO/RCED/AMID-99-88 (April).

———. 1999b. *Air Traffic Control: Observations on FAA's Air Traffic Control Modernization Program.* GAO/T-RCED/AMID-99-137 (March).

———. 2002. *Distribution of Airport Grant Funds Complied with Statutory Requirements.* GAO-02-283 (April).

GAO (United States Government Accountability Office). 2005a. *Aviation Fees: Review of Air Carriers' Year 2000 Passenger and Property Screening Costs.* GAO-05-558 (April).

———. 2005b. *Highway and Transit Investments: Options for Improving Information on Projects' Benefits and Costs and Increasing Accountability for Results.* GAO-05-172 (January).

———. 2006. *Intercity Passenger Rail: National Policy and Strategies Needed to Maximize Public Benefits from Federal Expenditures.* GAO-07-15 (November).

———. 2007. *Commercial Aviation: Programs and Options for Providing Air Service to Small Communities.* GAO-07-793T (April).

———. 2008. *TSA Has Developed a Risk-Based Covert Testing Program, but Could Better Mitigate Aviation Security Vulnerabilities Identified through Covert Tests.* GAO-08-958 (August).

———. 2009a. *DHS and TSA Have Researched, Developed, and Begun Deploying Passenger Checkpoint Screening Technologies, but Continue to Face Challenges.* GAO-10-128 (October).

———. 2009b. *High Speed Passenger Rail: Future Development Will Depend on Addressing Financial and Other Challenges and Establishing a Clear Federal Role.* GAO-09-317 (March).

Gaskins, Darius W. 2008. "Regulation of Freight Railroads in the Modern Era: 1970–2010." *Review of Network Economics* 7 (December): 561–72.

Gillen, David. 2001. "Assessing the Economic Benefits from the Implementation of New Pavement Construction Methods." *Transportation Research Record* 1747: 71–78.

Glaeser, Edward L., and Joshua Gottlieb. 2009. "The Wealth of Cities: Agglomeration Economies and Spatial Equilibrium in the United States." *Journal of Economic Literature* 47 (December): 983–1028.

Gomez-Ibanez, Jose A. 2003. *Regulating Infrastructure: Monopoly, Contracts, and Discretion.* Harvard University Press.

———. 2006. "An Overview of the Options." In *Competition in the Railway Industry: An International Comparative Analysis*, edited by Jose A. Gomez-Ibanez and Gines de Rus, pp. 1–22. Cheltenham, U.K.: Edward Elgar.

Gomez-Ibanez, Jose A., and John R. Meyer. 1993. *Going Private: The International Experience with Transport Privatization.* Brookings.

———. 1998. "Privatizing and Deregulating Local Public Services: Lessons from Britain's Buses." In *Transport Policy*, edited by Kenneth J. Button and Roger Stough, pp. 317–29. Cheltenham, U.K.: Edward Elgar.

Graham, Anne. 2004. "The Regulation of U.S. Airports." In *The Economic Regulation of Airports*, edited by Peter Forsyth and others. Burlington, Vt.: Ashgate Publishing.

———. 2008. "Airport Planning and Regulation in the United Kingdom." In *Aviation Infrastructure Performance: A Study in Comparative Political Economy*, edited by Winston and de Rus, pp. 100–35. Brookings.

Green, Richard K. 2006. "Airports and Economic Development." Working Paper. George Washington University, Department of Finance.

Grimm, Curtis, and Clifford Winston. 2000. "Competition in the Deregulated Railroad Industry: Sources, Effects, and Policy Issues." In *Deregulation of Network Industries: What's Next?* edited by Sam Peltzman and Clifford Winston, pp. 41–71. Brookings.

Grush, Bern, and Gabriel Roth. 2008. "Paying for Roads in the 21st Century with TDP Pricing." Paper 09-0222, presented at the 88th Annual Meeting of the Transportation Research Board, Washington, January.

Haltiwanger, John, Ron S. Jarmin, and Javier Miranda. 2010. "Who Creates Jobs? Small vs. Large vs. Young." Working Paper. University of Maryland (March).

Hilton, George. 1966. "The Consistency of the Interstate Commerce Act." *Journal of Economics* 9 (October): 87–113.

———. 1985. "The Rise and Fall of Monopolized Transit." In *Urban Transit: The Private Challenge to Public Transportation*, edited by Charles Lave, pp. 31–48. Cambridge, Mass.: Ballinger.

Hughes, Mark. 1994. "Mass Transit Agencies: Deregulating Where the Rubber Meets the Road?" In *Deregulating the Public Service: Can Government Be Improved?* edited by John J. Diulio, pp. 236–48. Brookings.

Hussain, Sajjad, and Neville A. Parker. 2006. "Pavement Damage and Road Pricing." Conference CD Paper 06-1342, presented at the 85th Annual Meeting of the Transportation Research Board, Washington, January.

Hymel, Kent. 2009. "Does Traffic Congestion Reduce Employment Growth?" *Journal of Urban Economics* 65 (March): 127–35.

Ishii, Jun, Sunyoung Jun, and Kurt Van Dender. 2008. "Air Travel Choices in Multi-Airport Markets." OECD Working Paper. Paris: Organization for Economic Cooperation and Development (November).

Jones, Charles I., and Paul M. Romer. 2010. "The New Kaldor Facts: Ideas, Institutions, Population, and Human Capital." *American Economic Journal: Macroeconomics* 2 (January): 224–45.

Kahn, Alfred E. 1988. "Surprises of Airline Deregulation." *American Economic Review* 78 (May): 316–22.

———. 1989. "Comment." *Brookings Papers on Economic Activity: Microeconomics:* 115–21.

Karlaftis, Matthew G. 2006. "Privatization, Regulation and Competition: A Thirty-Year Perspective on Transit Efficiency." Round Table 138 Report. Paris: OECD–European Conference of Ministers of Transport.

Karlaftis, Matthew, and Patrick McCarthy. 1999. "The Effect of Privatization on Public Transit Costs." *Journal of Regulatory Economics* 16 (July): 27–43.

Keeler, Theodore E. 1984. "Theories of Regulation and the Deregulation Movement." *Public Choice* 44 (January): 103–45.

Kessler, Daniel P., and Lawrence F. Katz. 2001. "Prevailing Wage Laws and Construction Labor Markets." *Industrial and Labor Relations Review* 54 (January): 259–74.

King, David, Michael Manville, and Donald Shoup. 2007. "For Whom the Road Tolls: The Politics of Congestion Pricing." *Access* (Fall): 2–7.

Klein, Daniel B., and Gordon J. Fielding. 1992. "Private Toll Roads: Learning from the 19th Century." *Transportation Quarterly* 46 (July): 321–41.

Klein, Daniel, and John Majewski. 1988. "Private Profit, Public Good, and Engineering Failure: The Plank Roads of New York." Working Paper 8813. George Mason University, Institute of Humane Studies.

———. 2006. "America's Toll Road Heritage: The Achievements of Private Initiative in the Nineteenth Century." In *Street Smart: Competition, Entrepreneurship, and the Future of Roads*, edited by Gabriel Roth, pp. 277–303. Oakland, Calif.: Independent Institute.

Knight, Frank H. 1924. "Some Fallacies in the Interpretation of Social Costs." *Quarterly Journal of Economics* 38 (August): 582–606.

Krugman, Paul. 2009. "The Increasing Returns Revolution in Trade and Geography." *American Economic Review* 99 (June): 561–71.

Langer, Ashley, and Clifford Winston. 2008. "Toward a Comprehensive Assessment of Road Pricing Accounting for Land Use." *Brookings-Wharton Papers on Urban Affairs.*

Lave, Charles. 1991. "Measuring the Decline in Transit Productivity in the U.S." *Transportation Planning and Technology* 15 (Winter): 115–24.

———. 1998. "25 Years of U.S. Energy Policy Successes, Failures, and Some General Lessons for Public Policy." *Transportation Quarterly* 52 (Fall): 7–13.

Lee, Douglass B. 1982. "New Benefits from Efficient Highway User Charges." *Transportation Research Record* 858: 14–20.

Lepatner, Barry B., Timothy Jacobson, and Robert E. Wright. 2007. *Broken Buildings, Busted Budgets: How to Fix America's Trillion-Dollar Construction Industry.* University of Chicago Press.

Levine, Michael E. 1969. "Landing Fees and the Airport Congestion Problem." *Journal of Law and Economics* 12 (April): 79–108.

———. 1981. "Revisionism Revised? Airline Deregulation and the Public Interest." *Law and Contemporary Problems* 44 (Winter): 179–95.

———. 2007. "Congestion Pricing at New York Airports: Right Idea, but Can We Really Start Here and Now?" Policy Brief 66. Los Angeles: Reason Foundation (November).

Levinson, David. 2010. "Economic Development Impacts of High-Speed Rail." Working Paper, University of Minnesota, Department of Civil Engineering (May).

Levinson, Marc. 2006. *The Box: How the Shipping Container Made the World Smaller and the World Economy Bigger.* Princeton University Press.

MacAvoy, Paul W. 2000. *The Natural Gas Market: Sixty Years of Regulation and Deregulation.* Yale University Press.

Makowsky, Michael D., and Thomas Stratmann. 2009. "Political Economy at Any Speed: What Determines Traffic Citations?" *American Economic Review* 99 (March): 509–27.

Mayer, Christopher, and Todd Sinai. 2003. "Network Effects, Congestion Externalities, and Air Traffic Delays: Or Why Not All Delays Are Evil." *American Economic Review* 93 (September):1194–215.

McDougall, Glen, and Alasdair Roberts. 2008. "Commercializing Air Traffic Control: Have the Reforms Worked?" *Canadian Public Administration Journal* 51 (March): 45–69.

Mead, Kenneth M. 2003. "Cost Control Issues for the Federal Aviation Administration's Operations and Modernization Accounts." Statement of the Inspector General of the Department of Transportation before the Committee on Appropriations, Subcommittee on Transportation, Treasury, and Independent Agencies, U.S. House of Representatives, April 9.

Megginson, William L., and Jeffrey M. Netter. 2001. "From State to Market: A Survey of Empirical Studies on Privatization." *Journal of Economic Literature* 39 (June): 321–89.

Meyer, John R., and Jose A. Gomez-Ibanez. 1981. *Autos, Transit, and Cities.* Harvard University Press.

Meyer, John R., and Clinton V. Oster Jr., with others. 1987. *Deregulation and the Future of Intercity Passenger Travel.* MIT Press.

Meyer, John, Merton J. Peck, John Stenason, and Charles Zwick. 1959. *The Economics of Competition in the Transportation Industries.* Harvard University Press.

Meyer, John R., and William B. Tye. 1988. "Toward Achieving Workable Competition in Industries Undergoing a Transition to Deregulation: A Contractual Equilibrium Approach." *Yale Journal on Regulation* 5 (July): 273–97.

Miller, Ted R., and Eduard Zaloshnja. 2009. "On a Crash Course: The Dangers and Health Costs of Deficient Roadways." Calverton, Md.: Pacific Institute for Research and Evaluation (May).

Moore, Adrian T., and Ted Balaker. 2006. "Do Economists Reach a Conclusion on Taxi Deregulation?" *Economic Journal Watch* 3 (January): 109–32.

Morrison, Steven A. 1983. "Estimation of Long-Run Prices and Investment Levels for Airport Runways," *Research in Transportation Economics* 1: 103–30.

———. 1990. "The Value of Amtrak." *Journal of Law and Economics* 33 (October): 361–82.

Morrison, Steven, and Clifford Winston. 1985. "An Econometric Analysis of the Demand for Intercity Passenger Transportation." *Research in Transportation Economics* 2: 213–37.

———. 1986. *The Economic Effects of Airline Deregulation.* Brookings.

———. 1989. "Enhancing the Performance of the Deregulated Air Transportation System." *Brookings Papers on Economic Activity: Microeconomics:* 61–123.

———. 1997. "The Fare Skies: Air Transportation and Middle America." *Brookings Review* (Fall): 42–45.

———. 1999. "Regulatory Reform of U.S. Intercity Transportation." In *Essays in Transportation Economics and Policy: A Handbook in Honor of John R. Meyer,* edited by Gomez-Ibanez, Tye, and Winston, pp. 469–92. Brookings.

———. 2000. "The Remaining Role for Government Policy in the Deregulated Airline Industry." In *Deregulation of Network Industries: What's Next?* edited by Peltzman and Winston, pp. 1–40. Brookings.

———. 2007. "Another Look at Airport Congestion Pricing." *American Economic Review* 97 (December): 1970–77.

———. 2008a. "Delayed! U.S. Aviation Infrastructure Policy at a Crossroads." In *Aviation Infrastructure Performance: A Study in Comparative Political Economy,* edited by Winston and Rus, pp. 7–35. Brookings.

————. 2008b. "The Effect of FAA Expenditures on Airport Delays." *Journal of Urban Economics* 63 (March): 669–78.

Morrison, Steven, Clifford Winston, and Vikram Maheshri. 2008. "Airline Competition and Travelers' Economic Welfare." Working Paper. Brookings.

Morrison, Steven, Clifford Winston, and Jia Yan. Forthcoming. "Airport Privatization and Travelers' Welfare." Working Paper. Brookings.

Moses, Fred, C. Schilling, and K. Raju. 1987. *Fatigue Evaluation Procedures for Steel Bridges.* Report 299. Washington: National Cooperative Highway Research Program (November).

Nash, Jonathan Remy. 2007. "Economic Efficiency versus Public Choice: The Case of Property Rights in Road Traffic Management." John M. Olin Program in Law and Economics Working Paper 374. University of Chicago Law School (December).

National Cooperative Highway Research Program. 2009. "Real-Time Traveler Information Programs." NCHRP Program Synthesis 399. Washington: Transportation Research Board.

National Surface Transportation Infrastructure Financing Commission. 2008. *The Path Forward: Funding and Financing Our Surface Transportation System.* Interim Report. Washington (February).

National Transportation Operations Coalition. 2007. "Executive Summary: 2007 National Traffic Signal Report Card." Washington.

Nelson, Peter, Andrew Baglino, Winston Harrington, Elena Safirova, and Abram Lipman. 2007. "Transit in Washington, DC: Current Benefits and Optimal Level of Provision." *Journal of Urban Economics* 62 (September): 231–51.

Ng, Chen Feng, and Kenneth A. Small. 2008. "Tradeoffs among Free-Flow Speed, Capacity, Cost, and Environmental Footprint in Highway Design." Working Paper. University of California, Irvine, Department of Economics (August).

Oster, Clinton V. Jr., with the assistance of John S. Strong. 2006. *Reforming the Federal Aviation Administration: Lessons from Canada and the United Kingdom.* Washington: IBM Center for the Business of Government.

O'Toole, Randal. 2006. "A Desire Named Streetcar: How Federal Subsidies Encourage Wasteful Local Transit Systems." *Policy Analysis.* Washington: Cato Institute (January).

————. 2009. "Getting What You Paid For—Paying for What You Get." *Policy Analysis.* Washington: Cato Institute (September).

————. 2010. "Defining Success: The Case against Rail Transit." *Policy Analysis.* Washington: Cato Institute (March).

Oum, Tae H., Jia Yan, and Chunyan Yu. 2008. "Ownership Forms Matter for Airport Efficiency: A Stochastic Frontier Investigation of Worldwide Airports." *Journal of Urban Economics* 64 (September): 422–35.

Pashigian, Peter. 1976. "Consequences and Causes of Public Ownership of Urban Transit Facilities." *Journal of Political Economy* 84 (December): 1239–59.

Peltzman, Sam. 1989. "The Economic Theory of Regulation after a Decade of Deregulation." *Brookings Papers on Economic Activity: Microeconomics:* 1–59.

Peoples, James. 1998. "Deregulation and the Labor Market." *Journal of Economic Perspectives* 12 (Summer): 111–30.

Perez, Benjamin G., with James W. March. 2006. "Public-Private Partnerships and the Development of Transport Infrastructure: Trends on Both Sides of the Atlantic."

Paper presented at the First International Conference on Funding Transportation Infrastructure, Banff, August (www.uofaweb.ualberta.ca/ipe/transportation conference2006.cfm).

Peterman, David Randall, John Frittelli, and William J. Mallett. 2009. *High Speed Rail (HSR) in the United States*. Washington: Congressional Research Service.

Pickrell, Don. 1990. *Urban Rail Transit Projects: Forecast versus Actual Ridership and Costs*. Washington: Urban Mass Transportation Administration.

Poole, Robert W. Jr., and Peter Samuel. 2008. "Pennsylvania Turnpike Alternatives." Policy Brief 70. Los Angeles: Reason Foundation (April).

Pozdena, Randall. 2009. "Driving the Economy: Automotive Travel, Economic Growth, and the Risks of Global Warming Regulations." Manzanita, Ore.: Quant Econ, Inc. (November).

Robyn, Dorothy. 1987. *Breaking the Special Interests: Trucking Deregulation and the Politics of Policy Reform*. University of Chicago Press.

——. 2007. "Reforming the Air Traffic Control System to Promote Efficiency and Reduce Delays." Paper prepared for the Council of Economic Advisors in association with GRA, Inc. (September).

Roden, Neil. 2006. "Development of Highway Concessions on Trunk Roads in the United Kingdom." In *Street Smart: Competition, Entrepreneurship, and the Future of Roads*, edited by Roth, pp. 399–421.

Roland, Gerard. 2008. "Private and Public Ownership in Economic Theory." In *Privatization: Successes and Failures*, edited by Gerard Roland, 9–31. Columbia University Press.

Roth, Gabriel. 2005. "Liberating the Roads: Reforming U.S. Highway Policy." Policy Analysis 538. Washington: Cato Institute (March).

——. 2006. "Why Involve the Private Sector in the Provision of Roads?" In *Street Smart: Competition, Entrepreneurship, and the Future of Roads*, edited by Roth, pp. 3–21.

Samuel, Peter, Robert W. Poole Jr., and Jose Holguin-Veras. 2002. "Toll Truckways: A New Path toward Safer and More Efficient Freight Transportation." Policy Study 294. Los Angeles: Reason Foundation (June).

Savage, Ian. 1999. "The Economics of Commercial Transportation Safety." In *Essays in Transportation Economics and Policy: A Handbook in Honor of John R. Meyer*, edited by Gomez-Ibanez, Tye, and Winston, pp. 531–62.

Savas, E. S., and E. J. McMahon. 2002. "Competitive Contracting of Bus Service: A Better Deal for Riders and Taxpayers." Civic Report 30. New York: Manhattan Institute (November).

Schaller, Bruce. 2010. "New York City's Congestion Pricing Experience and Implications for Road Pricing Acceptance in the United States." *Transport Policy* 17 (August): 266–73.

Schmidt, Steven. "Incentive Effects of Expanding Federal Mass Transit Formula Grants." *Journal of Policy Analysis and Management* 20 (Spring): 239–61.

Schwieterman, Joseph P. 2007. "The Return of the Intercity Bus: The Decline and Recovery of Scheduled Service to American Cities, 1960–2007." Policy study. DePaul University, School of Public Service (December).

Scovel, Calvin L. III. 2008. "Status of FAA's Efforts to Develop the Next Generation Air Transportation System." Statement of the U.S. Department of Transportation inspector general before the Committee on Science and Technology, U.S. House of Representatives, September 11, 2008.

Semmens, John. 2006. "De-Socializing the Roads." In *Street Smart: Competition, Entrepreneurship, and the Future of Roads*, edited by Roth, pp. 25–41.

Semmens, John, and Jeff Romine. 2006. "Price Trends for Major Roadway Inputs." Final Report 622. Phoenix: Arizona Department of Transportation (December).

Shirley, Chad, and Clifford Winston. 2004. "Firm Inventory Behavior and the Returns from Highway Infrastructure Investments." *Journal of Urban Economics* 55 (March): 398–415.

Shoup, Donald. 2005. *The High Cost of Free Parking.* Chicago: Planners Press.

Small, Kenneth A. 1999. "Economies of Scale and Self-financing Rules with Non-Competitive Factor Markets." *Journal of Public Economics* 74 (December): 431–50.

Small, Kenneth A., and Erik T. Verhoef. 2007. *The Economics of Urban Transportation.* London: Routledge Publishers.

Small, Kenneth A., Clifford Winston, and Carol A. Evans. 1989. *Road Work: A New Highway Pricing and Investment Policy.* Brookings.

Small, Kenneth A., Clifford Winston, and Jia Yan. 2005. "Uncovering the Distribution of Motorists' Preferences for Travel Time and Reliability." *Econometrica* 73 (July): 1367–82.

———. 2006. "Differentiated Road Pricing, Express Lanes, and Carpools: Exploiting Heterogeneous Preferences in Policy Design." *Brookings-Wharton Papers on Urban Affairs:* 53–96.

Starkie, David. 2001. "Reforming UK Airport Regulation." *Journal of Transport Economics and Policy* 35 (January): 119–35.

———. 2008a. "The Airport Industry in a Competitive Environment: A United Kingdom Perspective." OECD Discussion Paper 2008-15. Paris: Organization for Economic Cooperation and Development (July).

———. 2008b. *Aviation Markets: Studies in Competition and Regulatory Reform.* Burlington, Vt.: Ashgate Publishing.

Stevens, Henrik. 1999. *The Institutional Position of Seaports: An International Comparison.* Boston: Kluwer Academic Publishers.

Stewart, M. G., and J. Mueller. 2008. "Assessing the Risks, Costs and Benefits of United States Aviation Security Measures." Report 267.04.08. University of Newcastle, Center for Infrastructure Performance and Reliability.

Stigler, George J. 1965. "The Economist and the State." *American Economic Review* 55 (March): 1–18.

Stiglitz, Joseph E. 1998. "The Private Uses of Public Interests: Incentives and Institutions." *Journal of Economic Perspectives* 12 (Spring): 3–22.

Thieblot, A. J. 1996. "A New Evaluation of the Impacts of Prevailing Wage Law Repeal." *Journal of Labor Research* 17 (Spring): 297–322.

Todd, Kenneth. 2004. "Traffic Control: An Exercise in Self-Defeat." *Regulation* (Fall): 10–12.

United States Department of Transportation. 2006. *National Strategy to Reduce Congestion on America's Transportation Network* (May).

———. 2007. *Report to Congress on the Costs, Benefits, and Efficiencies of Public-Private Partnerships for Fixed Guideway Capital Projects* (November).

United States Federal Aviation Administration. 2000. "CY 2000 Passenger Boarding (Enplanement) and All-Cargo Data: Airport Hub Categories."

United States Federal Transit Administration. 2010. *National State of Good Repair Assessment* (June).

———. 2009. *Rail Modernization Study: Report to Congress* (April).

Utt, Ronald D. 2007. "Restoring Regional Equity to the Federal Highway Trust Fund." Backgrounder. Washington: Heritage Foundation (October).

———. 2008. "Bridge Repair Mismanagement Undermines Highway Safety." Web-Memo. Washington: Heritage Foundation (October).

Vickers, John, and George Yarrow. 1991. "Economic Perspectives on Privatization." *Journal of Economic Perspectives* 5 (Spring): 111–32.

Viton, Philip A. 1995. "Private Roads." *Journal of Urban Economics* 37 (May): 260–89.

Walters, A. A. 1982. "Externalities in Urban Buses." *Journal of Urban Economics* 11 (January): 60–72.

Wells, Alexander T. 1996. *Airport Management and Planning.* New York: McGraw-Hill.

Whalen, W. Tom, Dennis W. Carlton, Ken Heyer, and Oliver Richard. 2008. "A Solution to Airport Delays." *Regulation* 31 (Spring): 30–36.

Willis, Larry L. 2008. *Perryville Commuter.* Cleveland, Tenn.: Derek Press.

Winston, Clifford. 1998. "U.S. Industry Adjustment to Economic Deregulation." *Journal of Economic Perspectives* 12 (Summer): 89–110.

———. 2006. "The United States: Private and Deregulated." In *Competition in the Railway Industry: An International Comparative Analysis,* edited by Gomez-Ibanez and de Rus, pp. 135–52. Cheltenham, U.K.: Edward Elgar.

Winston, Clifford, Scott Dennis, and Vikram Maheshri. 2009. "Duopoly Equilibrium over Time in the Railroad Industry." Working Paper. Brookings (September).

Winston, Clifford, and Ashley Langer. 2006. "The Effect of Government Highway Spending on Road Users' Congestion Costs." *Journal of Urban Economics* 60 (November): 463–83.

Winston, Clifford and Vikram Maheshri. 2007. "On the Social Desirability of Urban Rail Transit Systems." *Journal of Urban Economics* 62 (September): 362–82.

Winston, Clifford, Vikram Maheshri, and Scott Dennis. Forthcoming. "Long-Run Effects of Mergers: The Case of U.S. Western Railroads." *Journal of Law and Economics.*

Winston, Clifford, and Chad Shirley. 1998. *Alternate Route: Toward Efficient Urban Transportation.* Brookings.

Winston, Clifford and Jia Yan. 2010. "U.S. Highway Privatization and Motorists' Heterogeneous Preferences." Working Paper. Brookings (March).

Wright, Robert E., and Brian P. Murphy. 2009. "The Private Provision of Transportation Infrastructure in Antebellum America: Lessons and Warnings." Working Paper (January) (http://ssrn.com/abstract=1335301).

Zhang, Anming, and Yimin Zhang. 2003. "Airport Charges and Capacity Expansion: Effects of Concessions and Privatization." *Journal of Urban Economics* 53 (January): 54–75.

Index

AASHTO. *See* American Association of State Highway and Transportation Officials

Acela high-speed rail, 32

ADS-B (Automatic Dependent Surveillance-Broadcast), 85–86, 160

Advani, Asheesh, 139

AHS (Automated highway systems), 58

AIP. *See* Airport Improvement Program

Air Canada, 78

Air Florida, 27

Airline Deregulation Act of 1978, 12, 114

Airlines: accidents, 76–77; competition in, 25–27; delays, 24, 25, 77–79, 121; deregulation of, 21–28, 109, 114, 115, 117, 119–20, 145; fares, 27, 113, 117, 119; load factors of, 23, 117, 118, 119; mergers of, 25–26; operations improvements in, 118; overbooking, 117, 122; passengers' bill of rights, 24, 25; safety issues, 27–28, 82, 100–101; service issues, 22–25; subsidies for, 22–23. *See also specific airlines*

Airport and Airway Improvement Act of 1982, 79–80

Airport and Airway Safety and Capacity Expansion Act of 1987, 22

Airport and Airway Trust Fund, 9–10, 80, 84, 98

Airport Development Program, 79

Airport Improvement Program (AIP), 9, 80, 81, 92

Airports: catchment areas of, 135; compensatory charging system, 80–81; concessions at, 138, 159; delays at, 87–90, 104–5, 121, 135; economic performance of, 86–95; gate utilization and access, 92–94; grants for, 81–82, 92; inefficiencies in, 100, 103; infrastructure and policy of, 79–82; investment in, 90–92; landing fees, 80, 87, 89; privatization of, 135–40, 143, 159; and public-private partnerships, 130; public sector involvement in, 9; runways, 86–92, 103, 138; security at, 25, 82–83, 94–97; slot system at, 88–89. *See also* Air traffic control; *specific airports*

Air route traffic control centers (ARTCCs), 83–84

Air traffic control: and delays, 97; economic performance of, 97–101; inefficiencies in, 24–25, 103; infrastructure and policy of, 83–86; investment in, 98–99; NextGen, 84–86, 99–100, 106, 160; and pricing, 97–98, 100, 105; privatization of, 140–42, 143, 160; public sector involvement in, 9–10; and technology, 84–86, 99–100, 106, 158

Air Traffic Control Center, 9

Air Traffic Organization (ATO), 76, 98, 99, 141

Air Tran, 27, 94

179